GRI™

Pick Of The Litter
by
Mike Peters

TOR
A TOM DOHERTY ASSOCIATES BOOK
NEW YORK

GRIMMY: PICK OF THE LITTER

A TOR Book
Published by Tom Doherty Associates, Inc.
49 West 24 Street
New York, NY 10010

ISBN: 0-812-51080-1

First Tor edition: December 1990

Printed in the United States of America

0 9 8 7 6 5 4 3 2 1

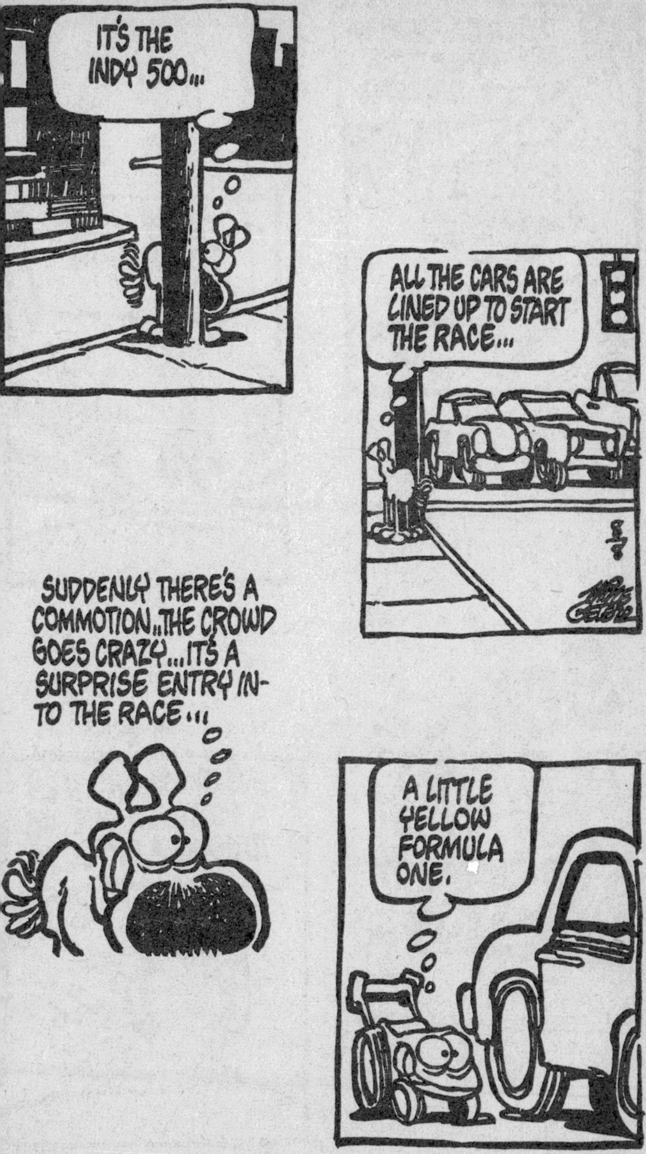
IT'S THE INDY 500...
ALL THE CARS ARE LINED UP TO START THE RACE...
SUDDENLY THERE'S A COMMOTION..THE CROWD GOES CRAZY...IT'S A SURPRISE ENTRY INTO THE RACE...
A LITTLE YELLOW FORMULA ONE.

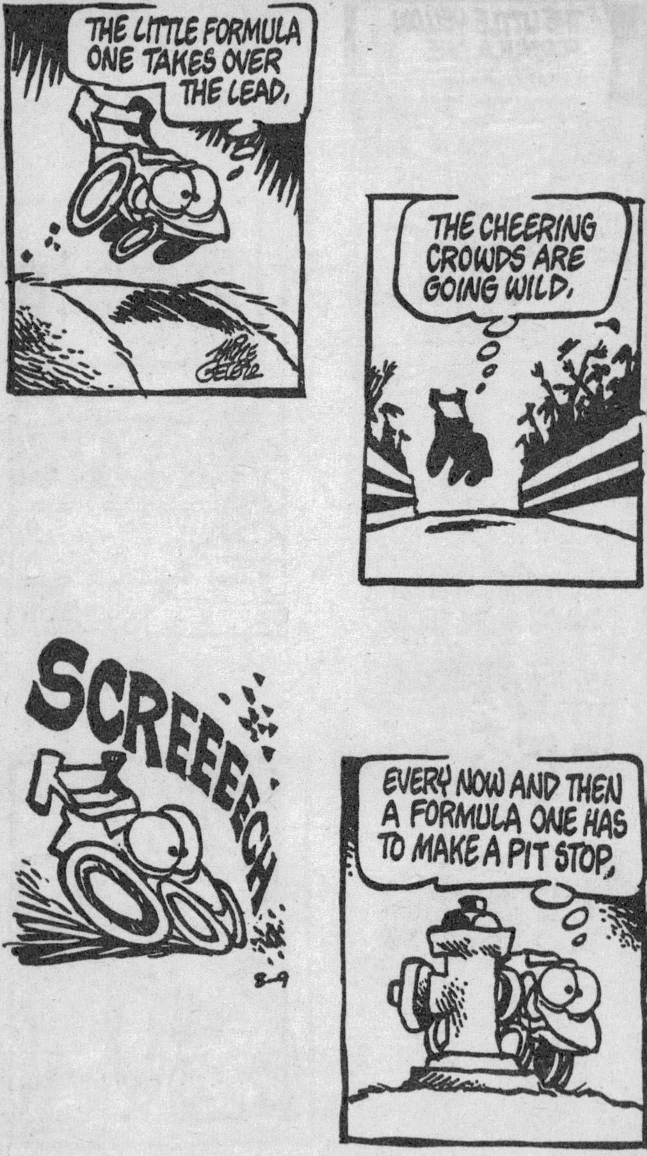
THE LITTLE FORMULA ONE TAKES OVER THE LEAD.
THE CHEERING CROWDS ARE GOING WILD.
SCREEEECH
8-9
EVERY NOW AND THEN A FORMULA ONE HAS TO MAKE A PIT STOP.

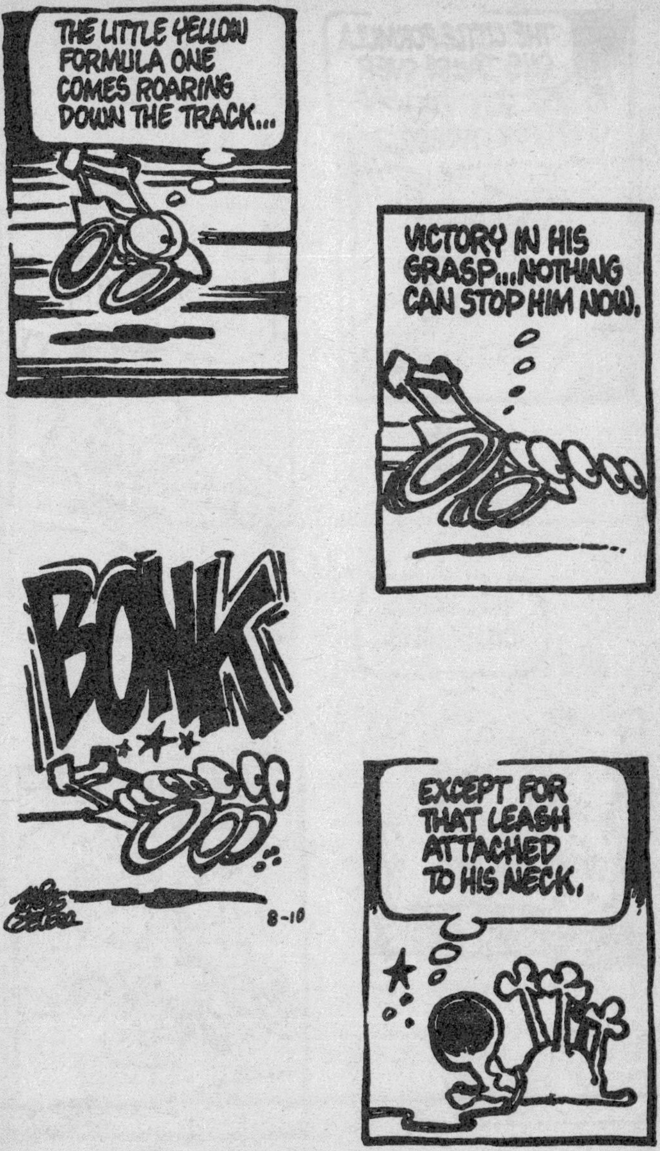
THE LITTLE YELLOW FORMULA ONE COMES ROARING DOWN THE TRACK...
VICTORY IN HIS GRASP...NOTHING CAN STOP HIM NOW.
BONK
EXCEPT FOR THAT LEASH ATTACHED TO HIS NECK.
8-10

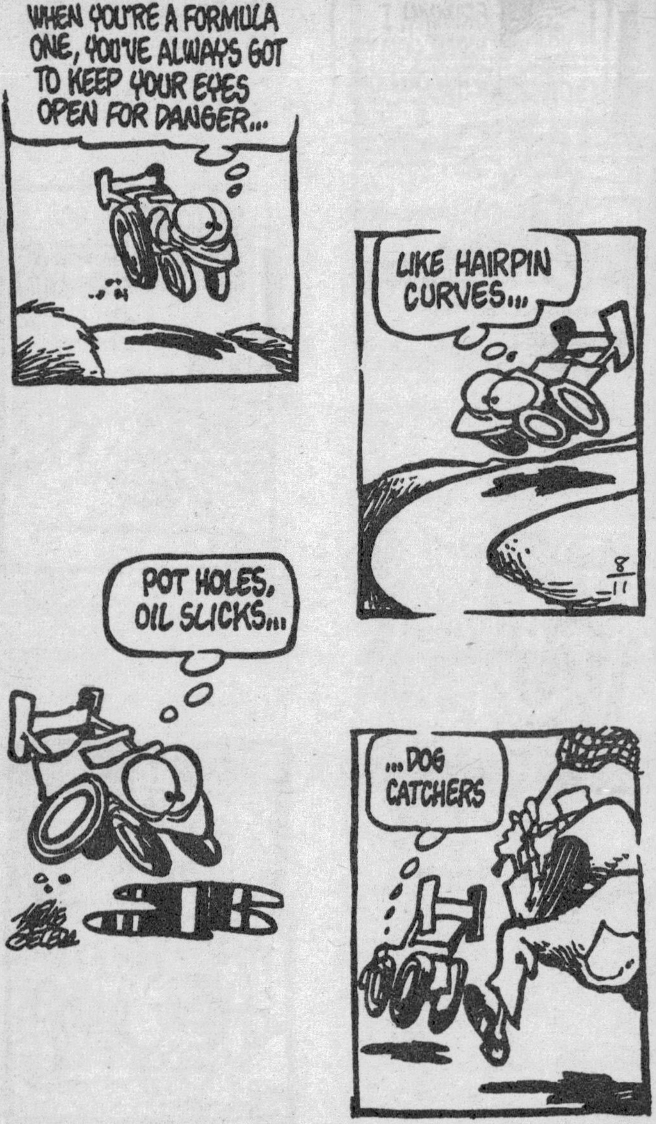
WHEN YOU'RE A FORMULA ONE, YOU'VE ALWAYS GOT TO KEEP YOUR EYES OPEN FOR DANGER...
LIKE HAIRPIN CURVES...
8/11
POT HOLES, OIL SLICKS...
...DOG CATCHERS

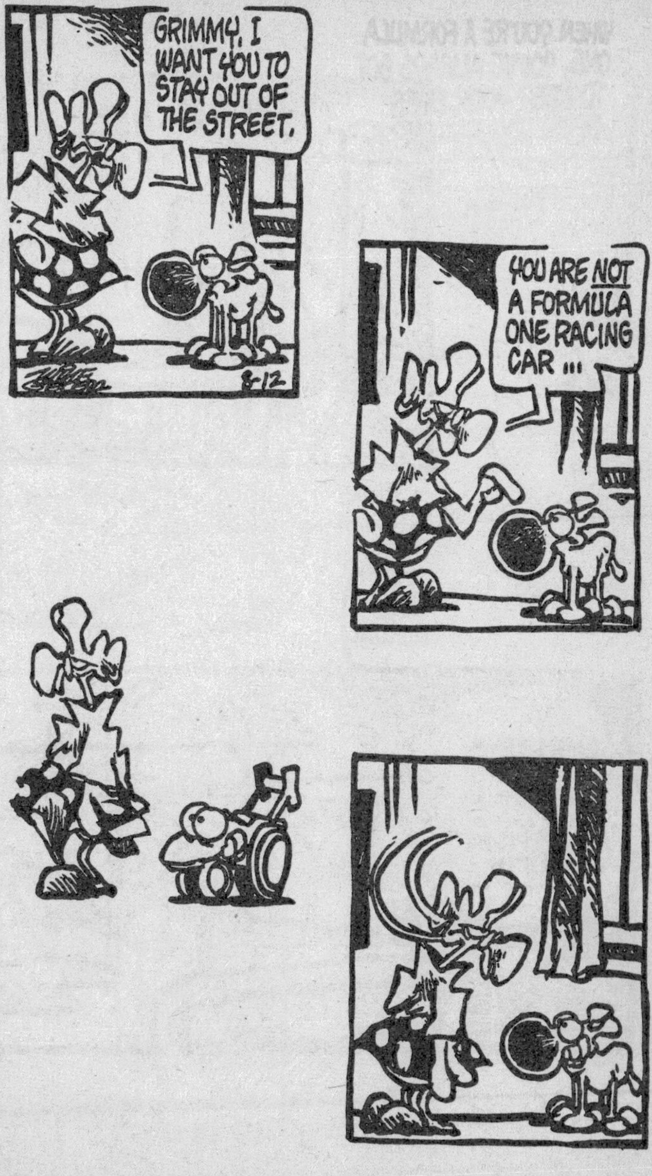
GRIMMY, I WANT YOU TO STAY OUT OF THE STREET.
8-12
YOU ARE NOT A FORMULA ONE RACING CAR ...

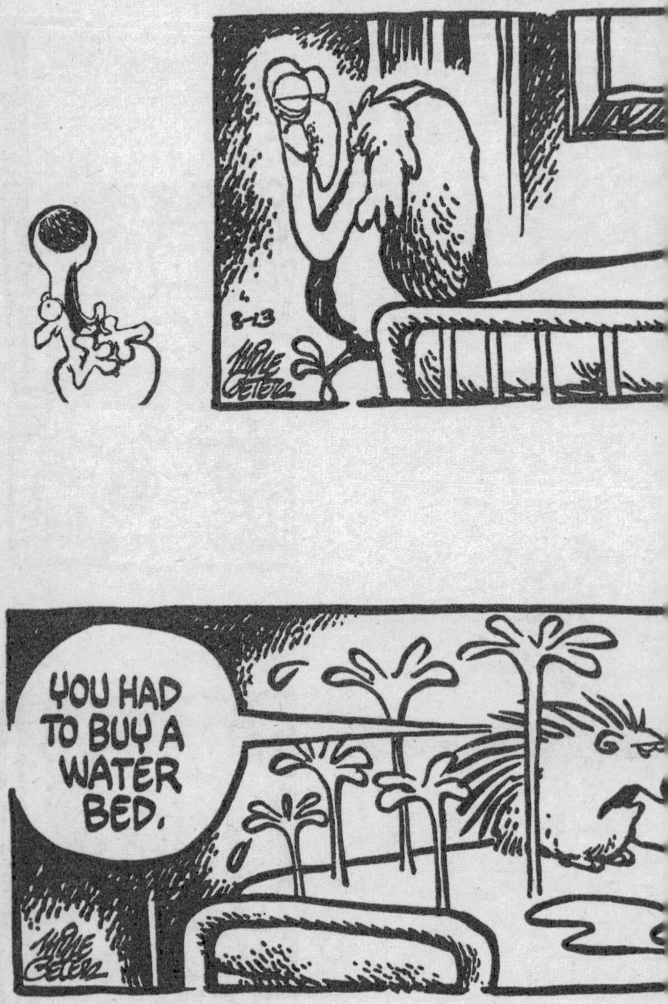
8-13
YOU HAD TO BUY A WATER BED.

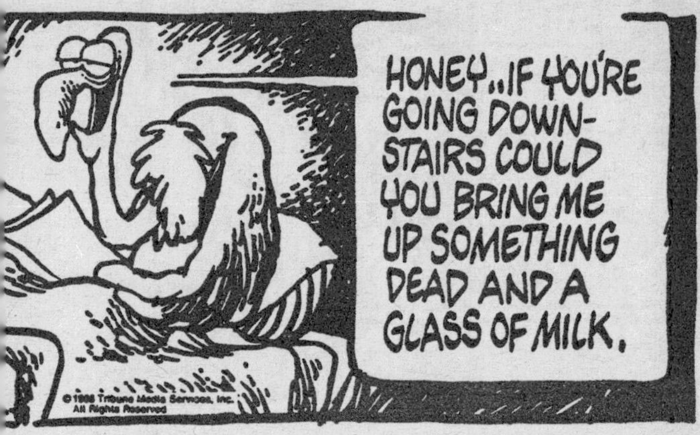
HONEY..IF YOU'RE GOING DOWN-STAIRS COULD YOU BRING ME UP SOMETHING DEAD AND A GLASS OF MILK.

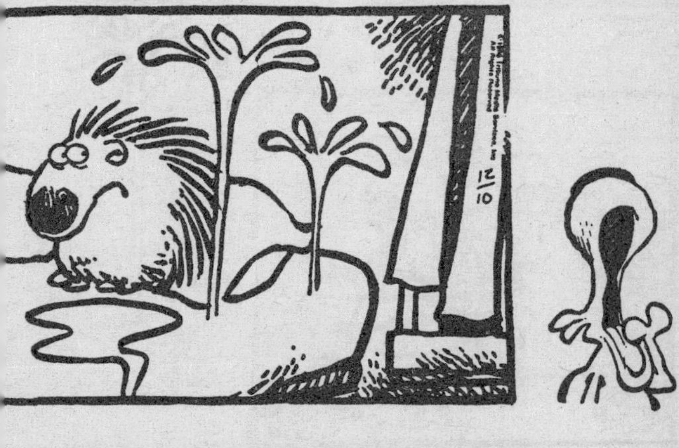
12/10

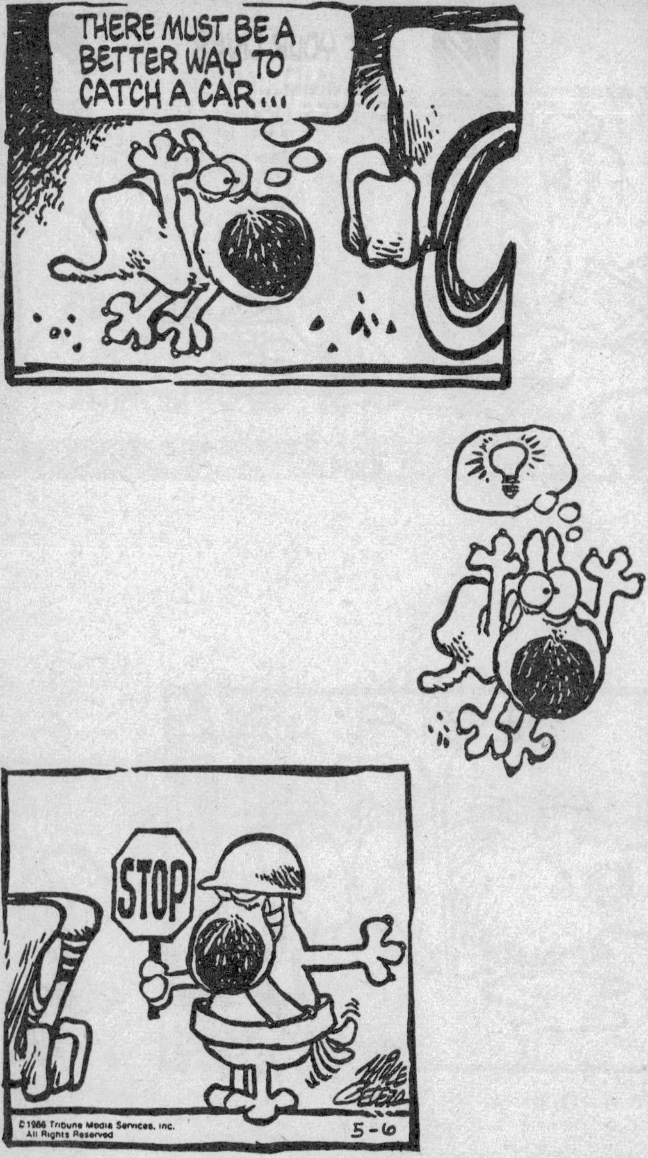
THERE MUST BE A BETTER WAY TO CATCH A CAR...
STOP
©1986 Tribune Media Services, Inc.
All Rights Reserved
5-6

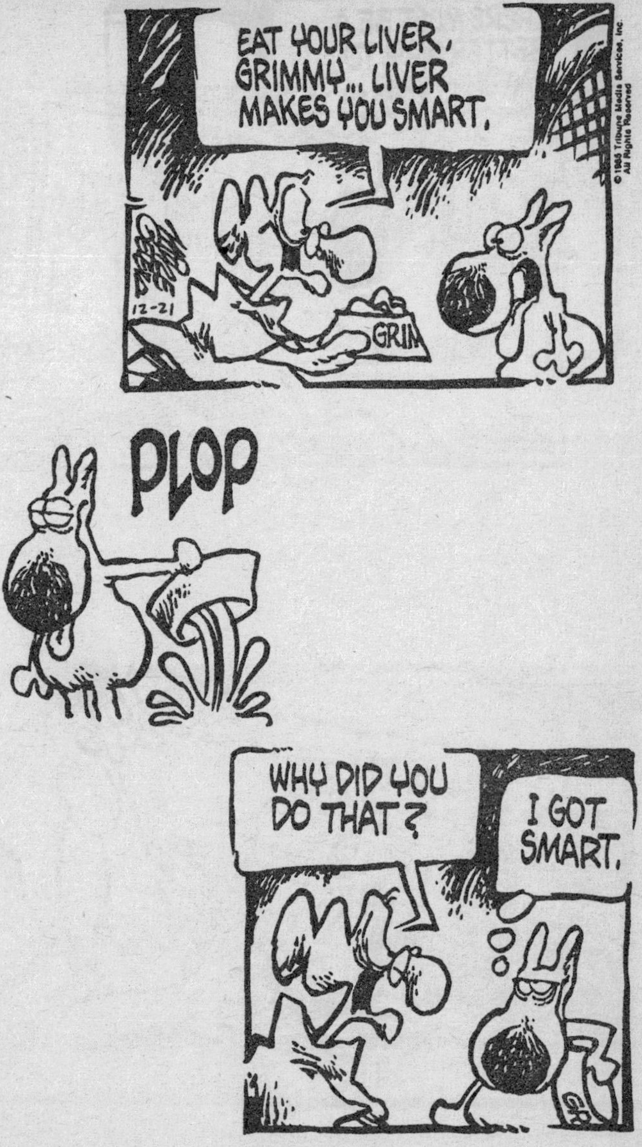
EAT YOUR LIVER, GRIMMY... LIVER MAKES YOU SMART.
12-21
GRIM
PLOP
WHY DID YOU DO THAT?
I GOT SMART.

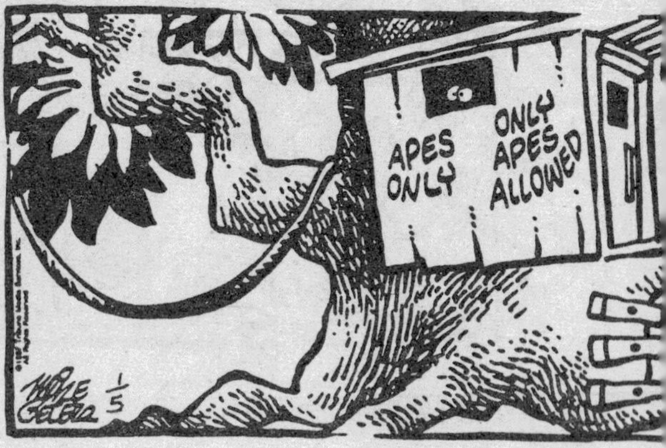
APES ONLY
ONLY APES ALLOWED
1/5

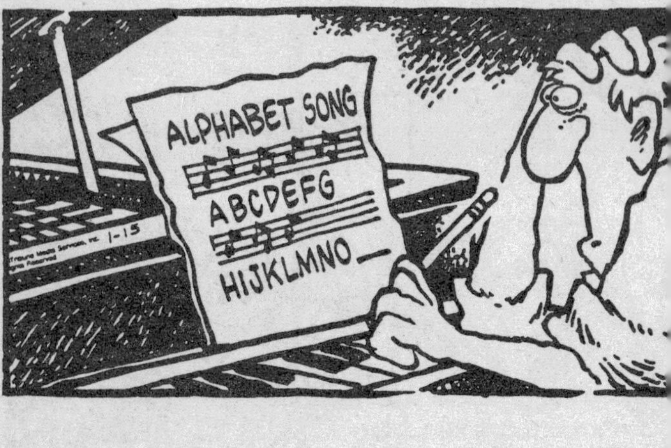
ALPHABET SONG
ABCDEFG
HIJKLMNO__
1-15

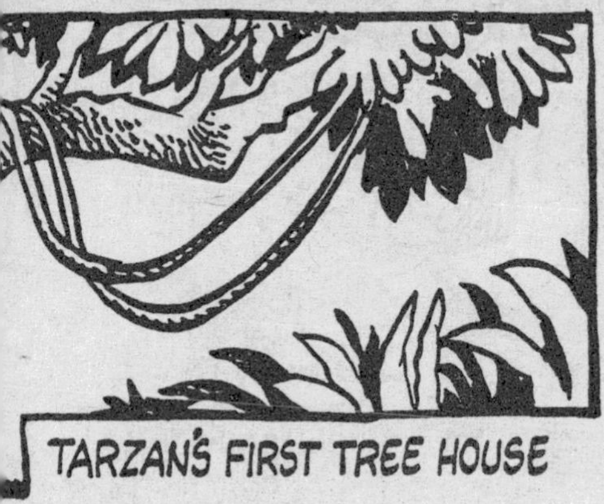
TARZAN'S FIRST TREE HOUSE

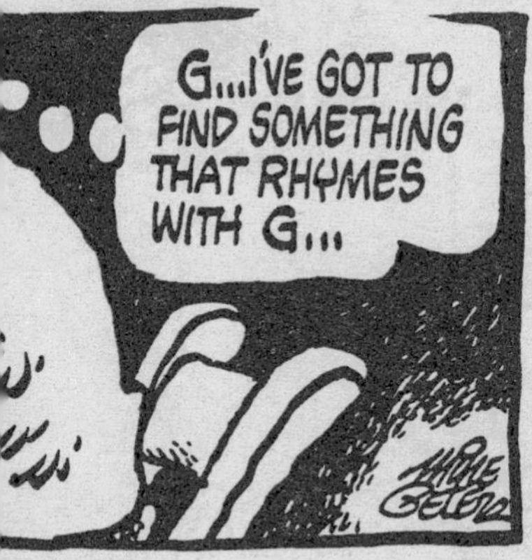
G...I'VE GOT TO FIND SOMETHING THAT RHYMES WITH G...
MIKE PETERS

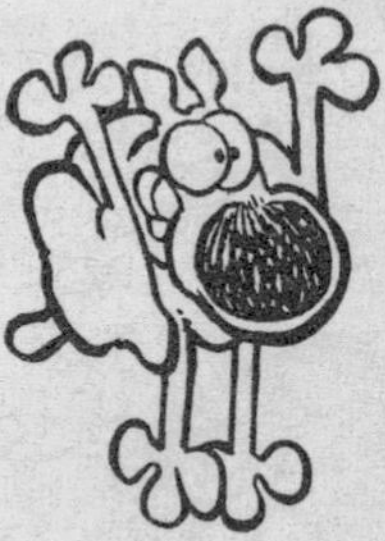

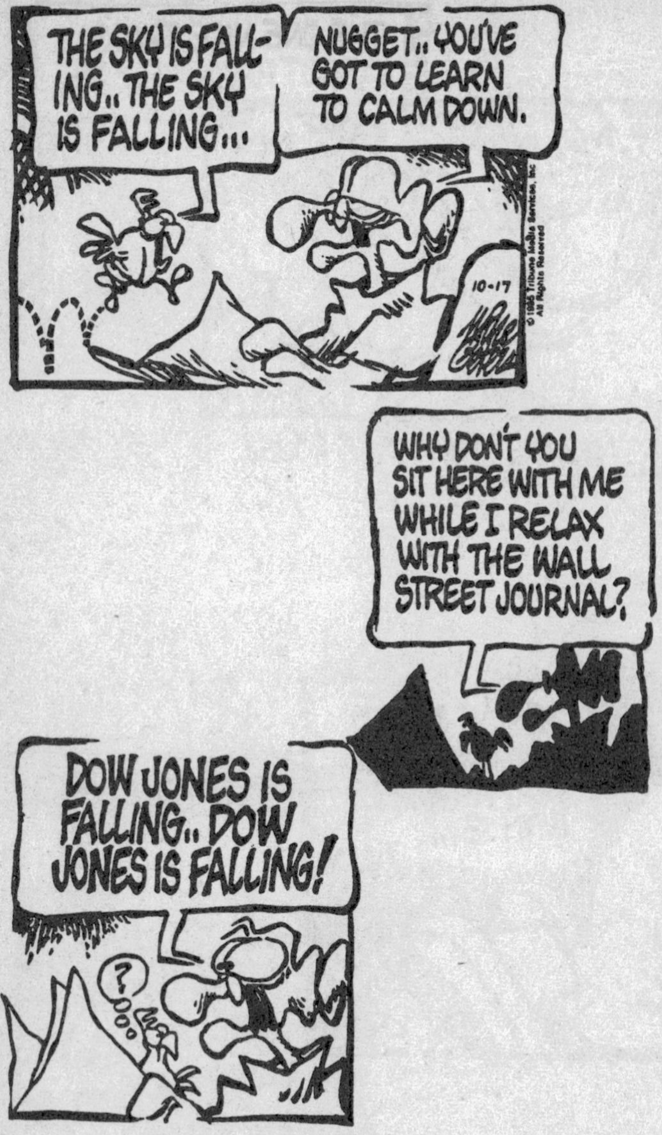
THE SKY IS FALL-ING.. THE SKY IS FALLING...
NUGGET.. YOU'VE GOT TO LEARN TO CALM DOWN.
10-17
WHY DON'T YOU SIT HERE WITH ME WHILE I RELAX WITH THE WALL STREET JOURNAL?
DOW JONES IS FALLING.. DOW JONES IS FALLING!
?

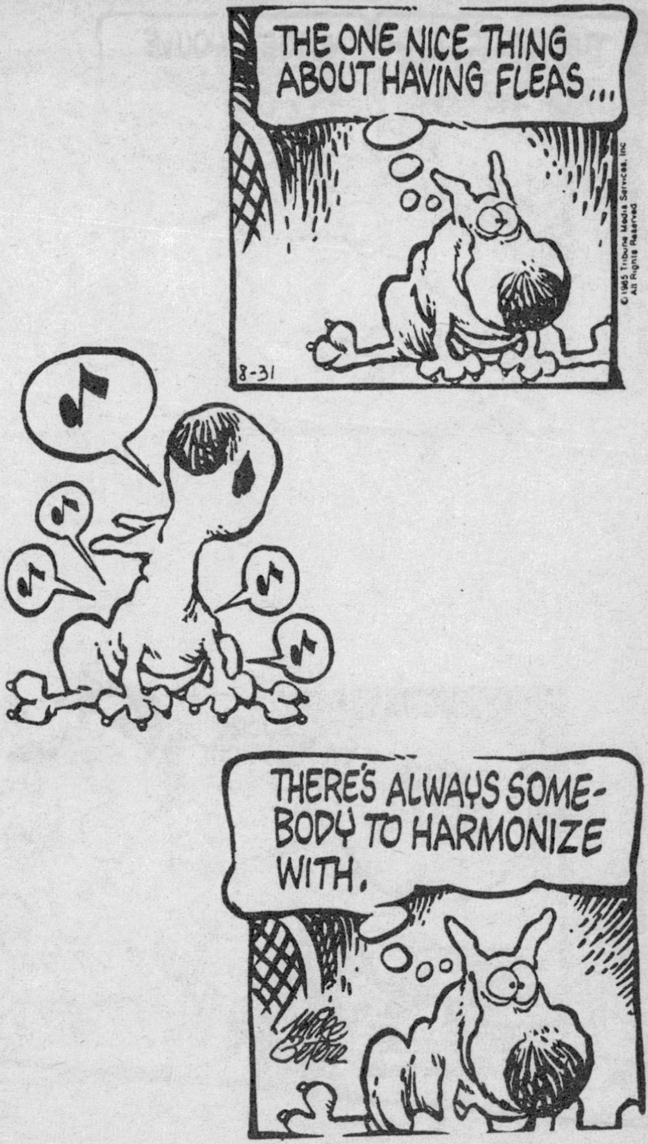
THE ONE NICE THING ABOUT HAVING FLEAS...
8-31
© 1985 Tribune Media Services, Inc
All Rights Reserved
THERE'S ALWAYS SOME-BODY TO HARMONIZE WITH.

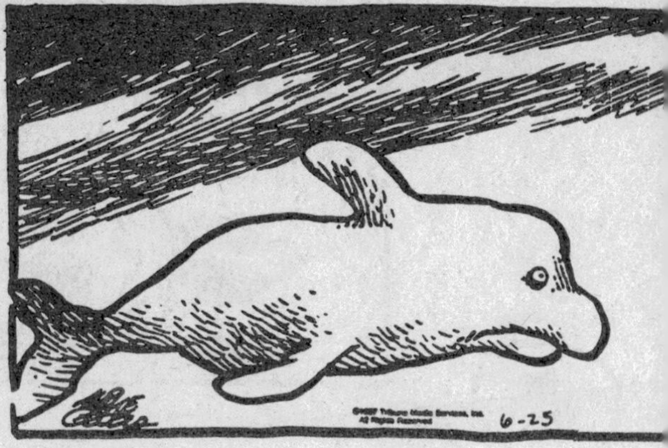
©1987 Tribune Media Services, Inc.
All Rights Reserved
6-25

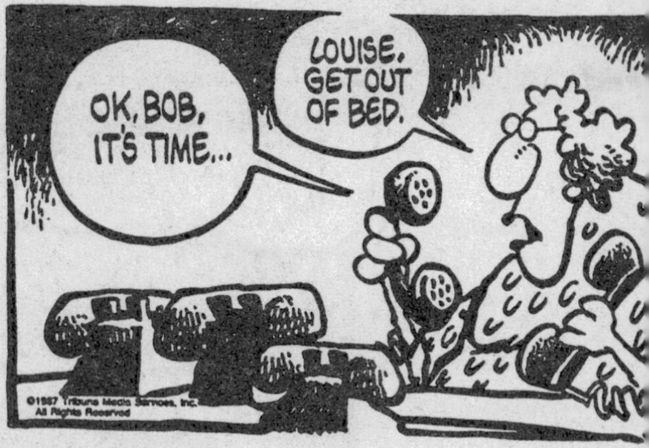
OK, BOB, IT'S TIME...
LOUISE, GET OUT OF BED.
©1987 Tribune Media Services, Inc.
All Rights Reserved

NO.. I USED TO BE A DOLPHIN.. BUT THEN I GOT TRADED TO THE RAIDERS.

EXCUSE YOURSELF, LEO...
HURRY, CARL,
11-19

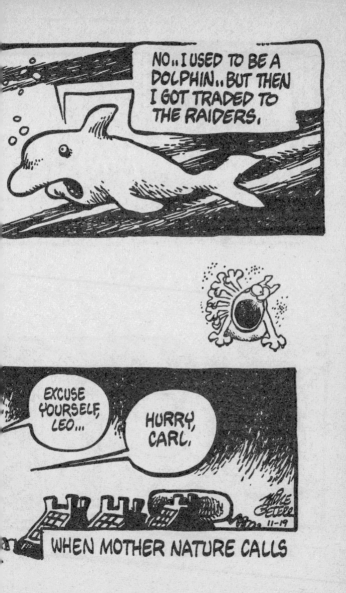

WHEN MOTHER NATURE CALLS

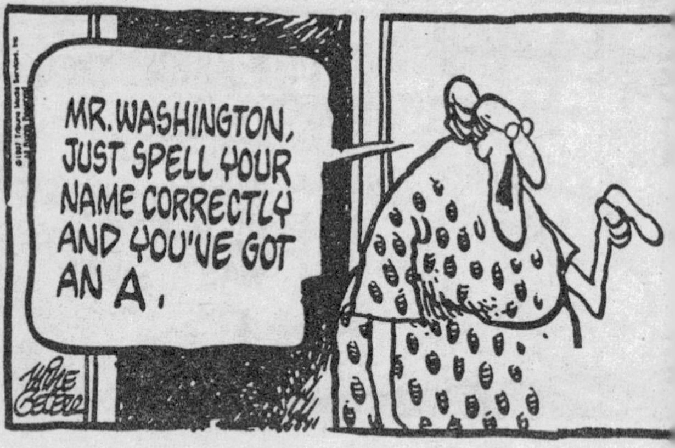
MR. WASHINGTON, JUST SPELL YOUR NAME CORRECTLY AND YOU'VE GOT AN A.

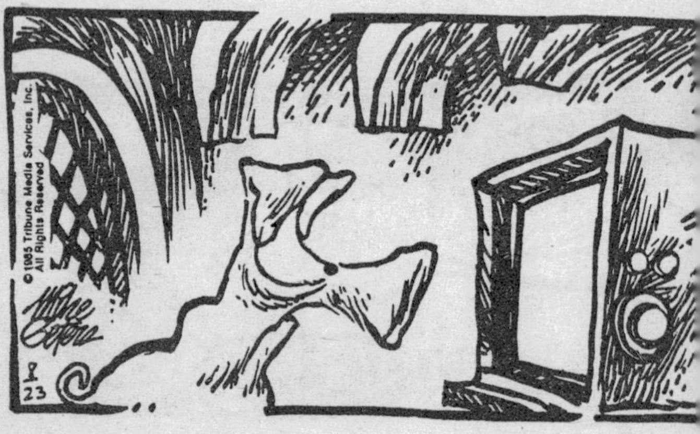
©1985 Tribune Media Services, Inc.
All Rights Reserved
8
23

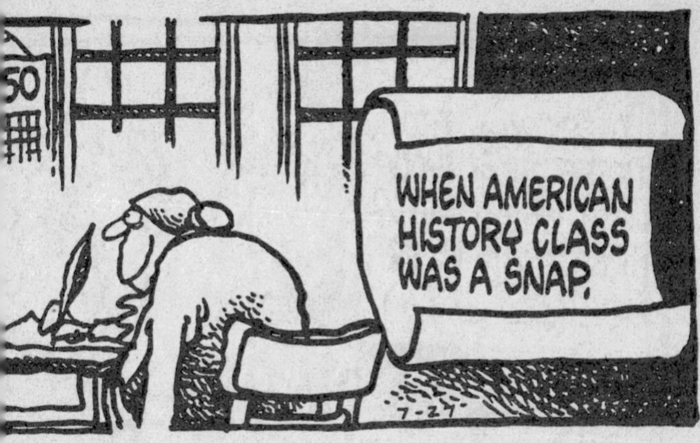
50
WHEN AMERICAN HISTORY CLASS WAS A SNAP.
7-27

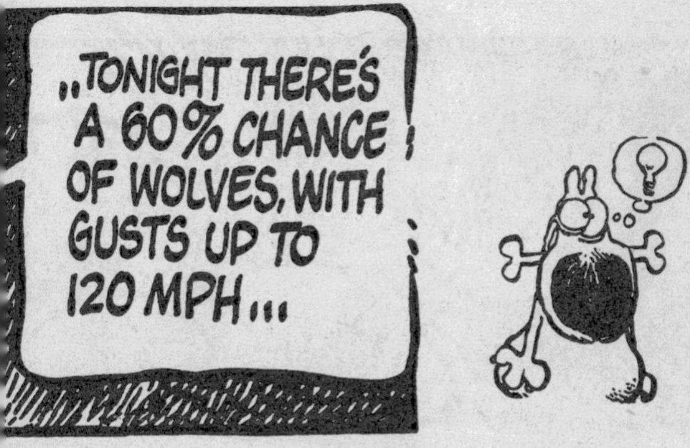
..TONIGHT THERE'S A 60% CHANCE OF WOLVES, WITH GUSTS UP TO 120 MPH...

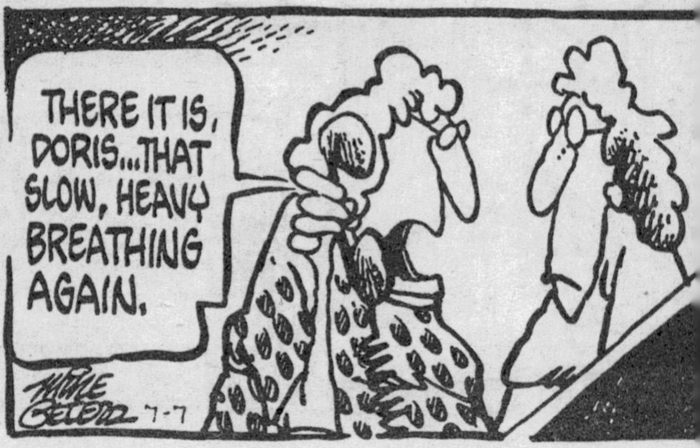
THERE IT IS, DORIS...THAT SLOW, HEAVY BREATHING AGAIN.
7-7

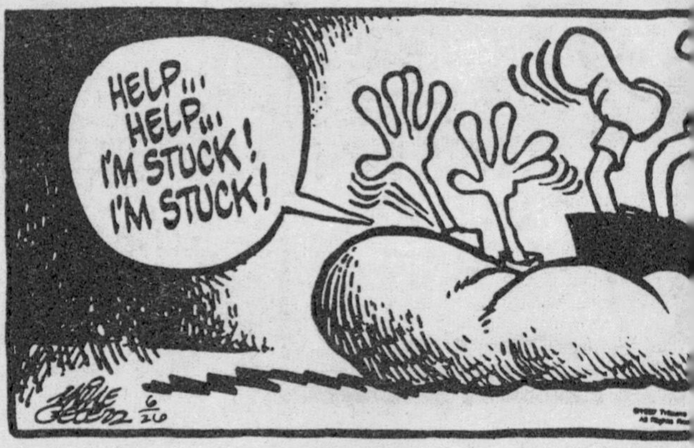
HELP... HELP... I'M STUCK! I'M STUCK!
6/26

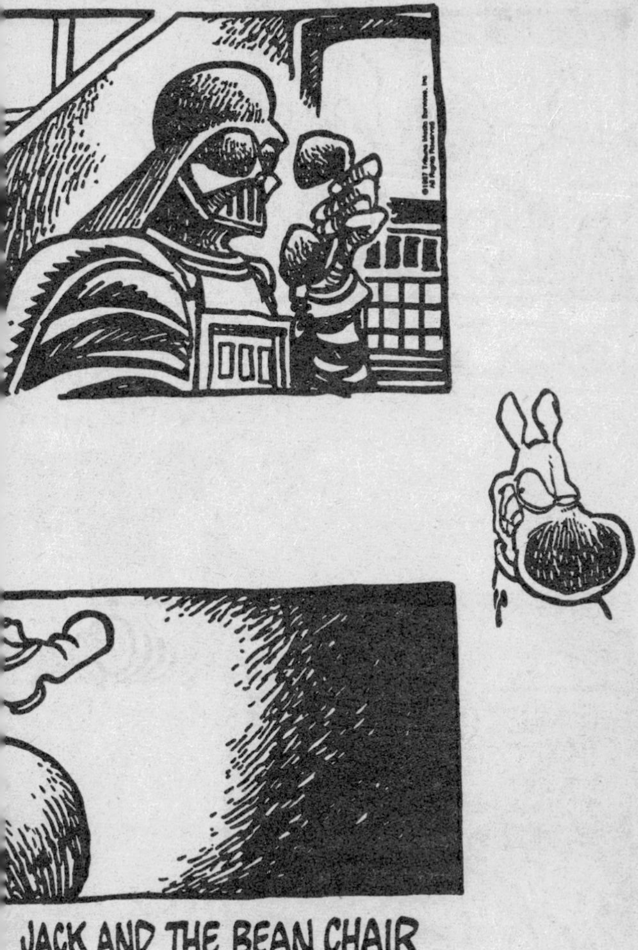

JACK AND THE BEAN CHAIR

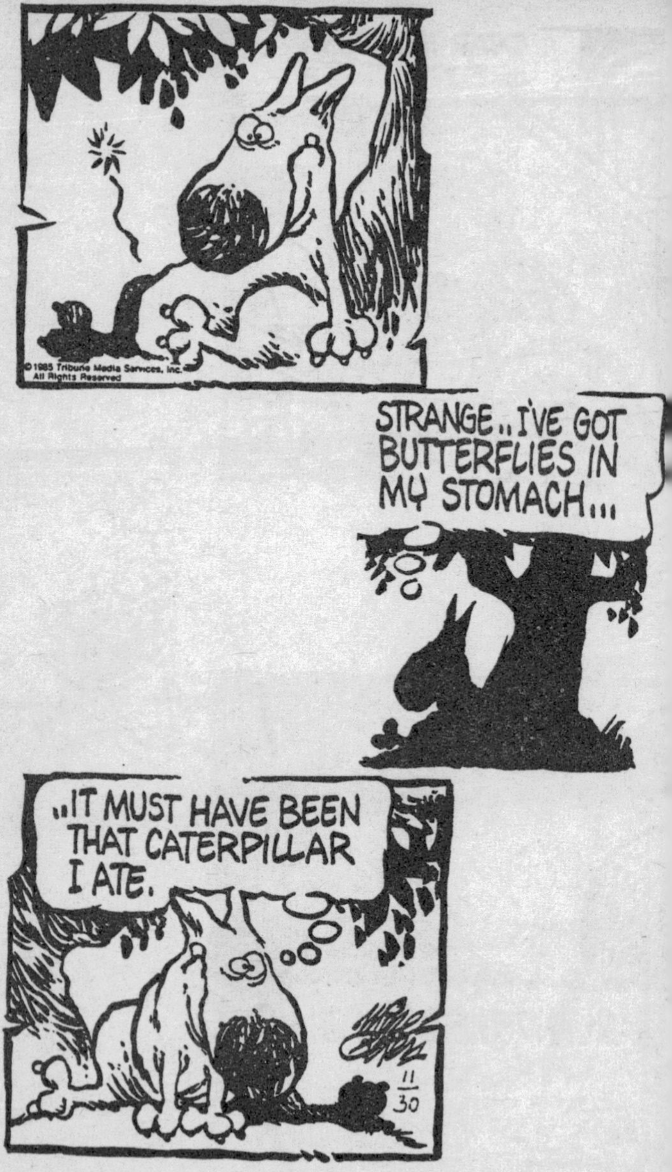
©1985 Tribune Media Services, Inc.
All Rights Reserved
STRANGE.. I'VE GOT BUTTERFLIES IN MY STOMACH...
..IT MUST HAVE BEEN THAT CATERPILLAR I ATE.
11/30

DEAR MZ GOOSE, IS IT TRUE THAT A DOG IS A MAN'S BEST FRIEND?
YES.
MAN'S GOT PROBLEMS.
9-27

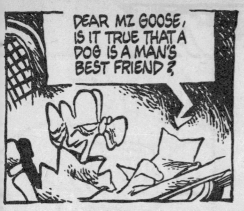

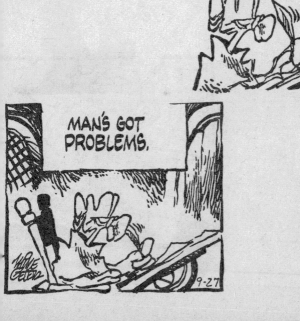

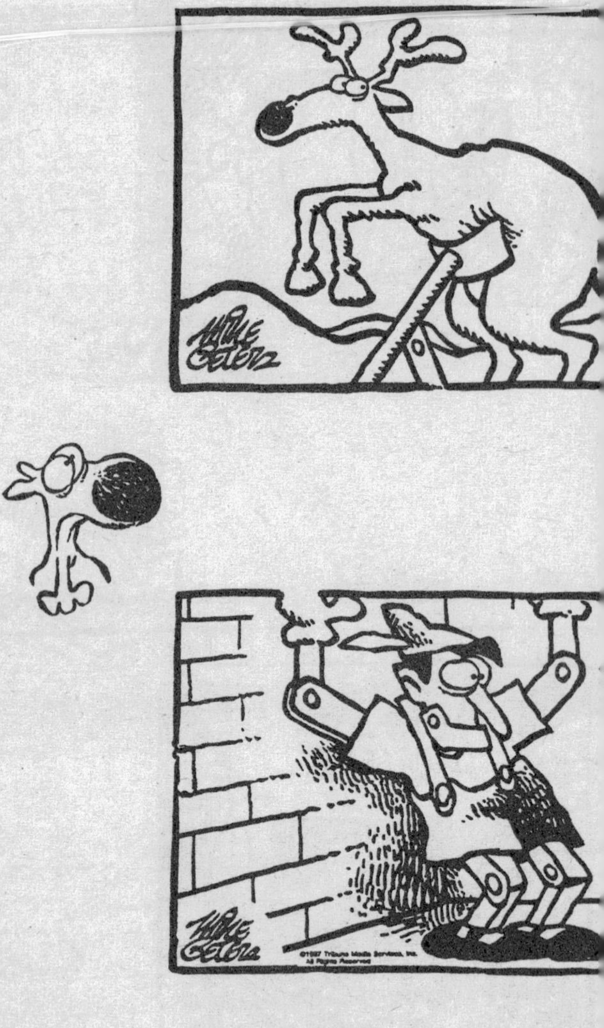
©1987 Tribune Media Services, Inc.
All Rights Reserved

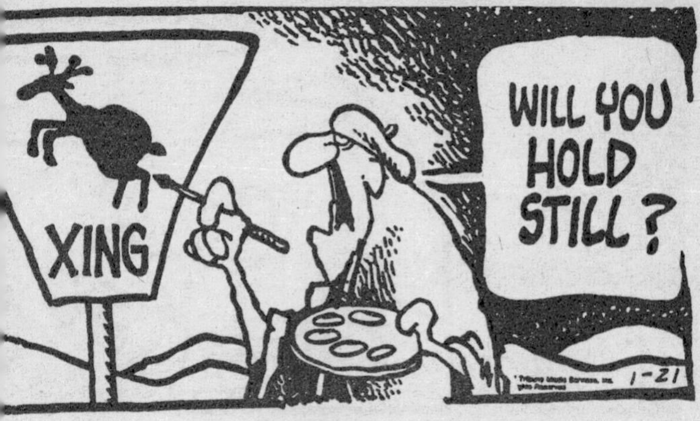
XING
WILL YOU HOLD STILL?
1-21

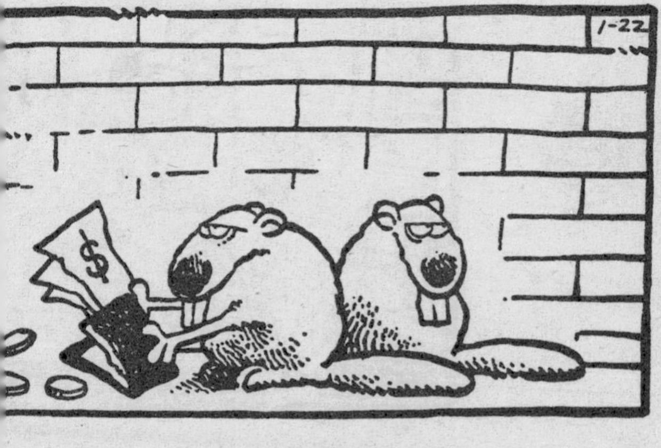
1-22
$

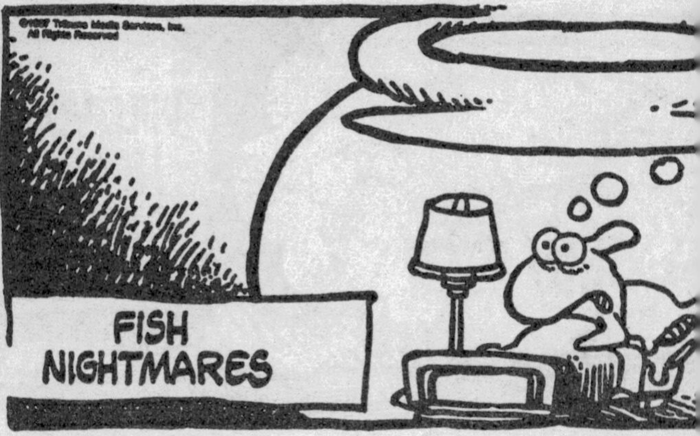

Tribune Media Services, Inc.
All Rights Reserved
FISH NIGHTMARES

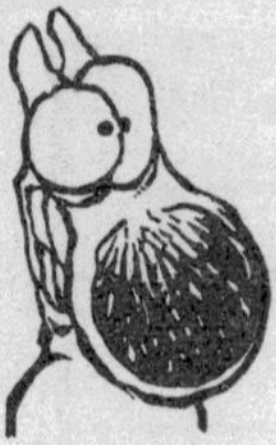

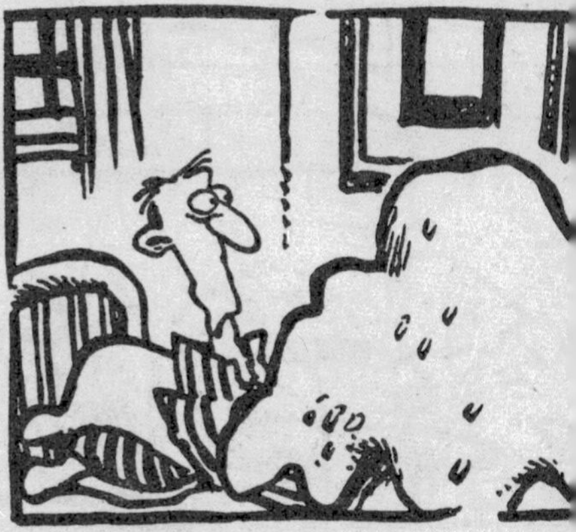

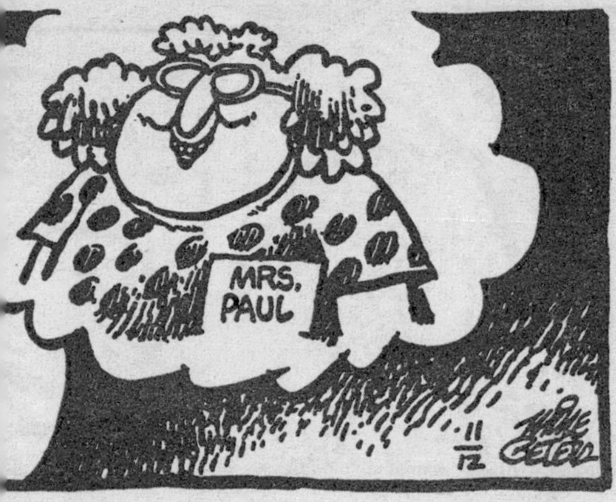
MRS.
PAUL
11
12

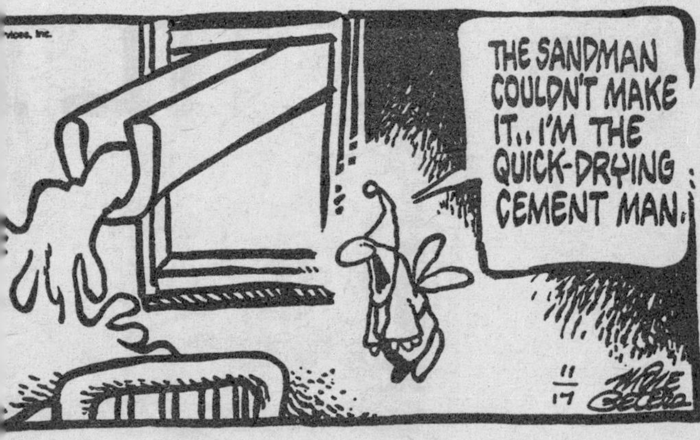
rvices, Inc.
THE SANDMAN COULDN'T MAKE IT.. I'M THE QUICK-DRYING CEMENT MAN.
11
17

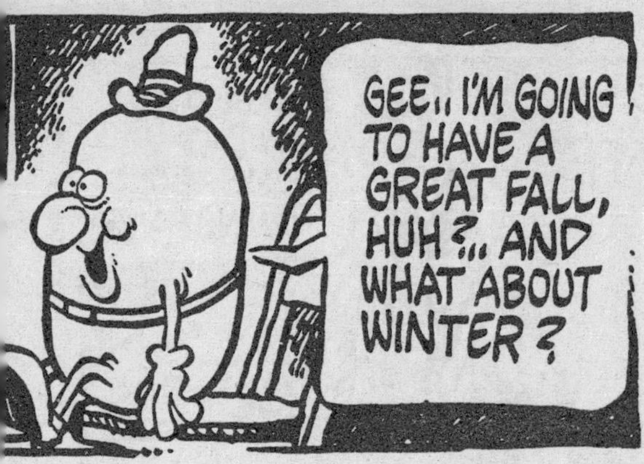
GEE.. I'M GOING TO HAVE A GREAT FALL, HUH?... AND WHAT ABOUT WINTER?

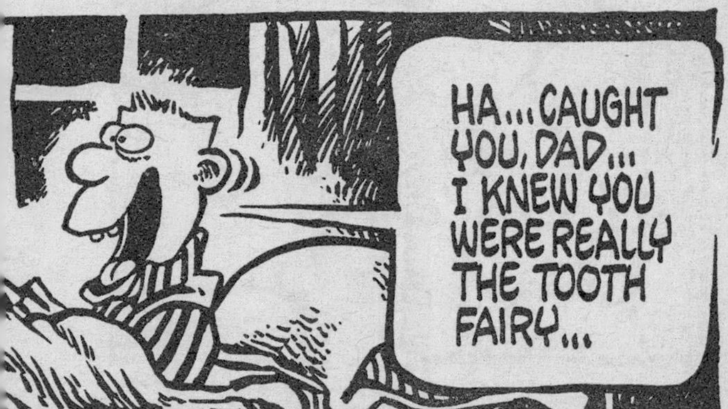
HA...CAUGHT YOU, DAD... I KNEW YOU WERE REALLY THE TOOTH FAIRY...

THERE'S ONLY ONE BAD THING ABOUT HAVING FANGS...
BITING YOUR TONGUE...
5-3

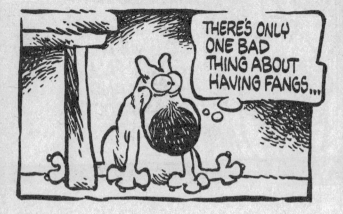

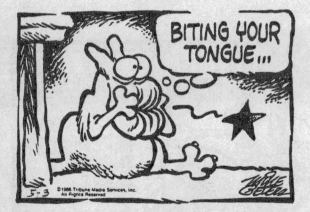

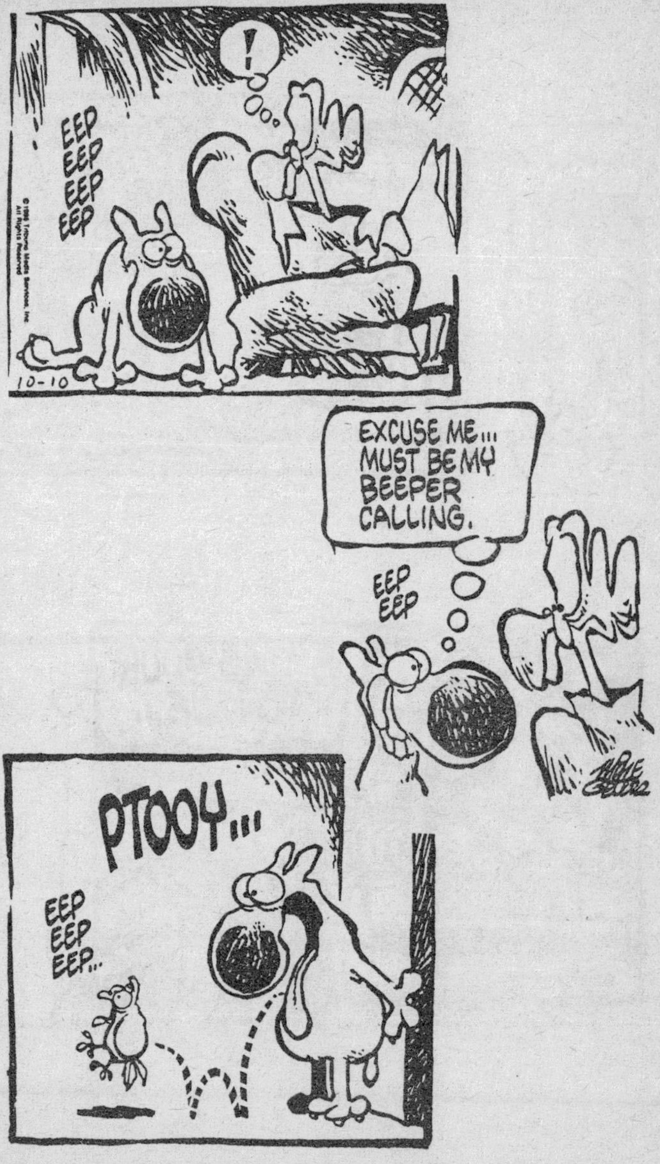
!
EEP EEP EEP EEP
10-10
EXCUSE ME... MUST BE MY BEEPER CALLING.
EEP EEP
PTOOY...
EEP EEP EEP...

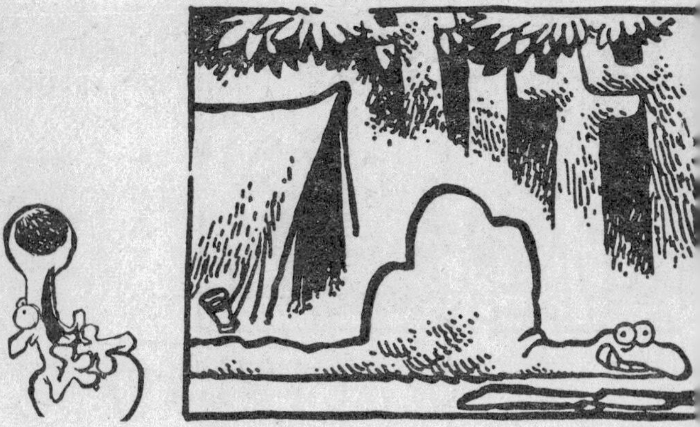

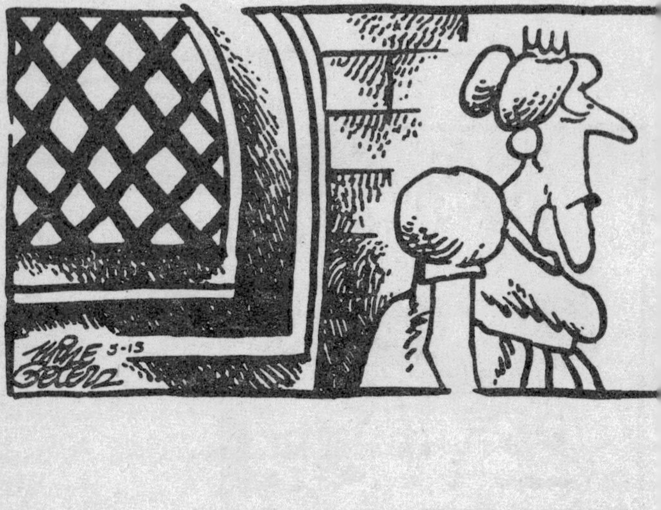
MIKE PETERS 5-13

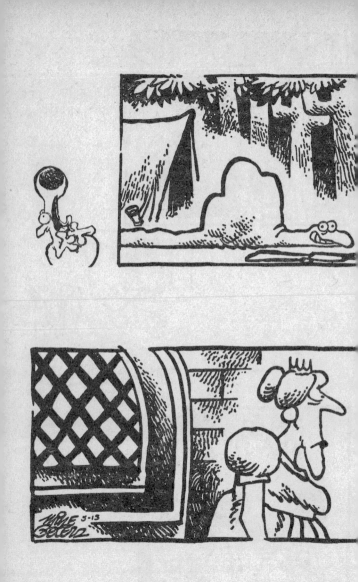

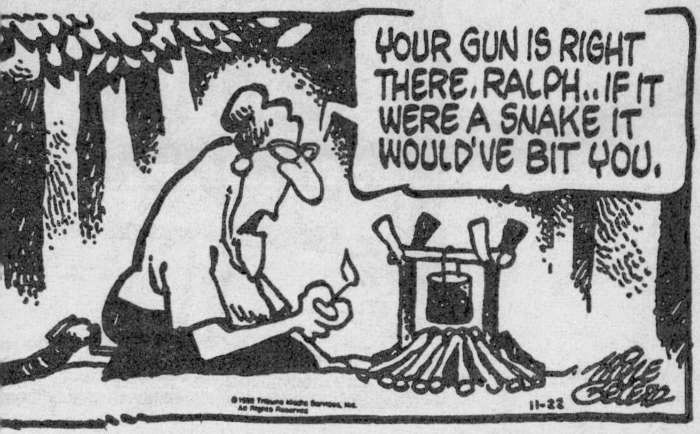
YOUR GUN IS RIGHT THERE, RALPH..IF IT WERE A SNAKE IT WOULD'VE BIT YOU.
11-22

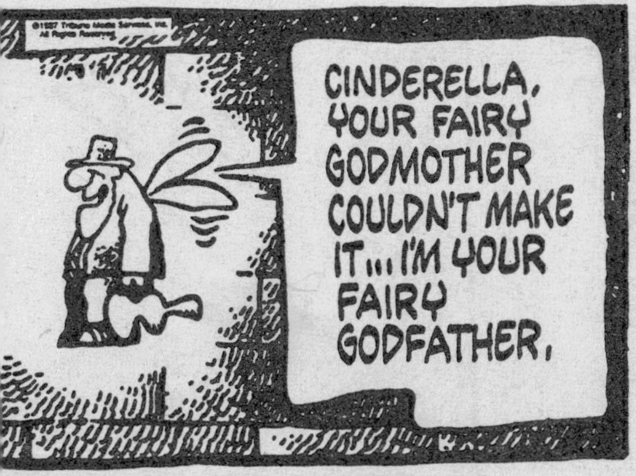
CINDERELLA, YOUR FAIRY GODMOTHER COULDN'T MAKE IT... I'M YOUR FAIRY GODFATHER.

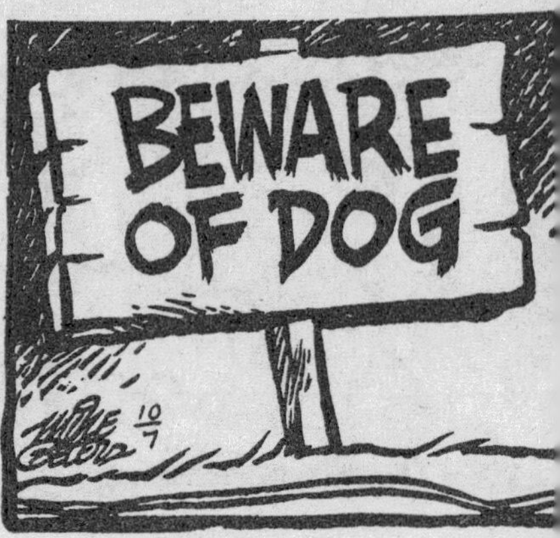
BEWARE
OF DOG

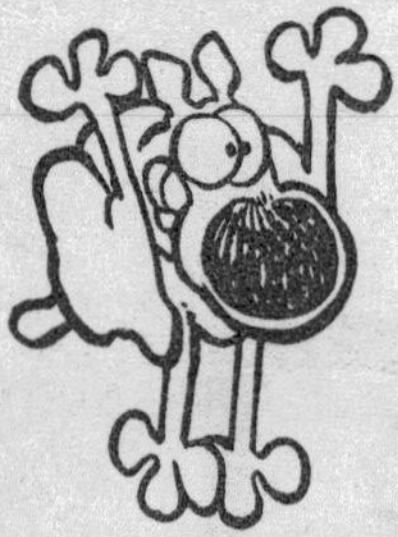

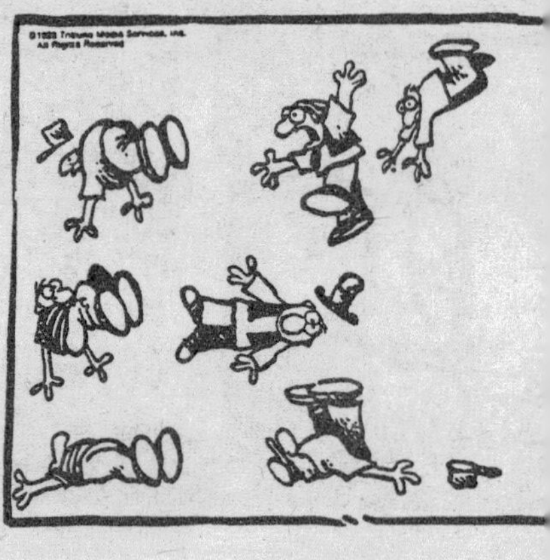

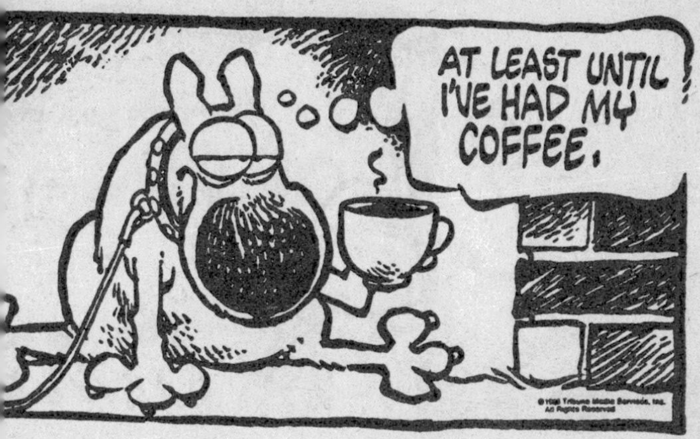
AT LEAST UNTIL I'VE HAD MY COFFEE.

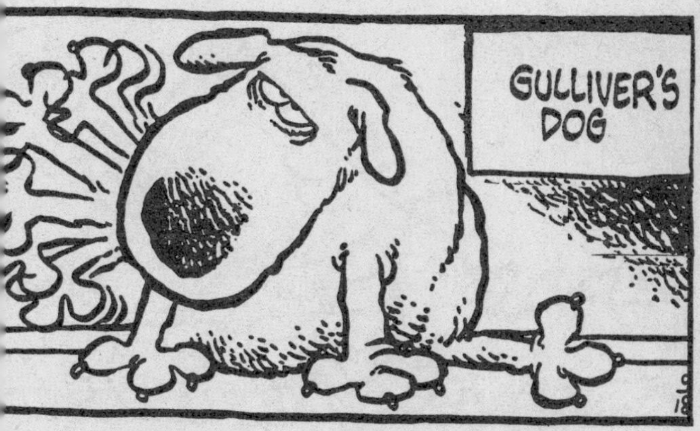
GULLIVER'S DOG

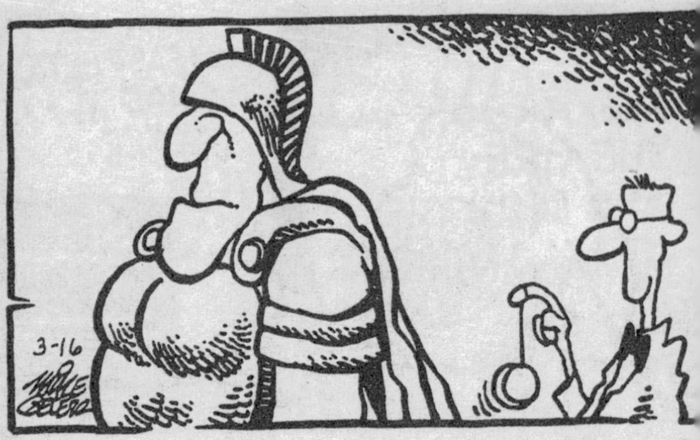
3-16

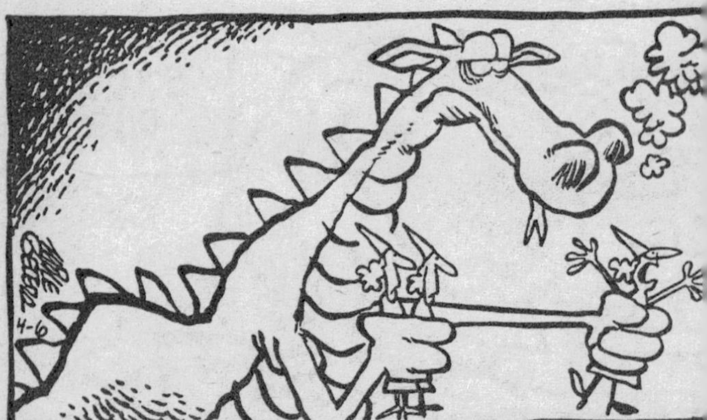
4-6

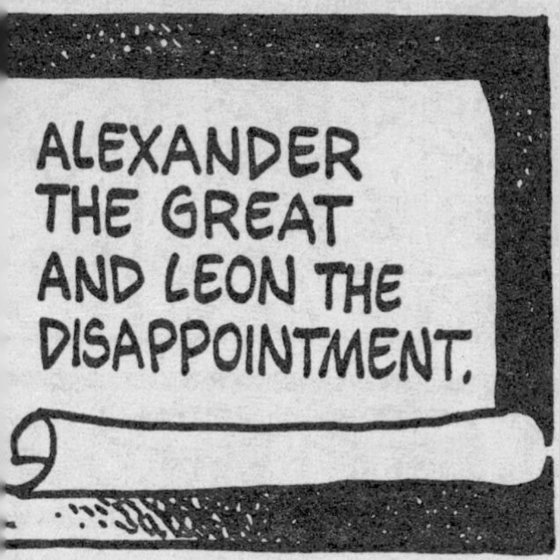
ALEXANDER THE GREAT AND LEON THE DISAPPOINTMENT.

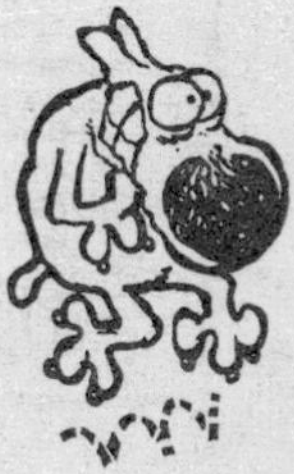

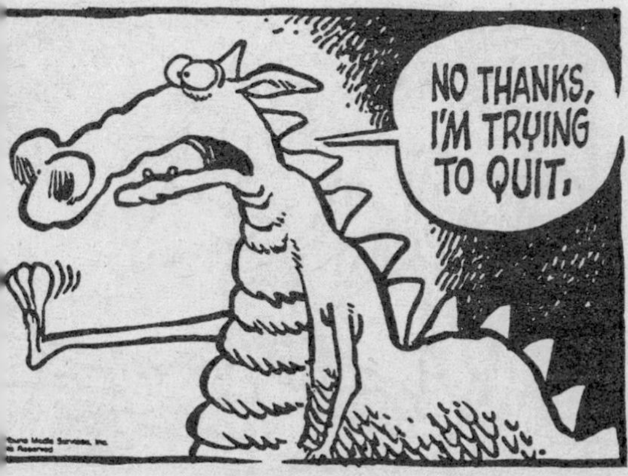
NO THANKS, I'M TRYING TO QUIT.

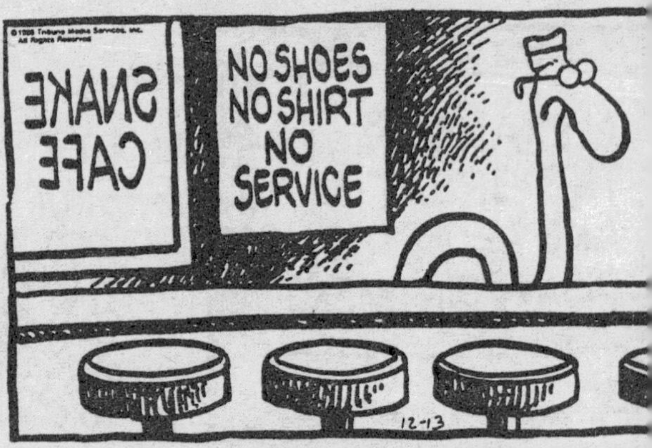
SNAKE CAFE
NO SHOES NO SHIRT NO SERVICE
12-13

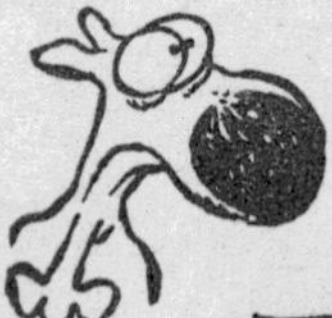

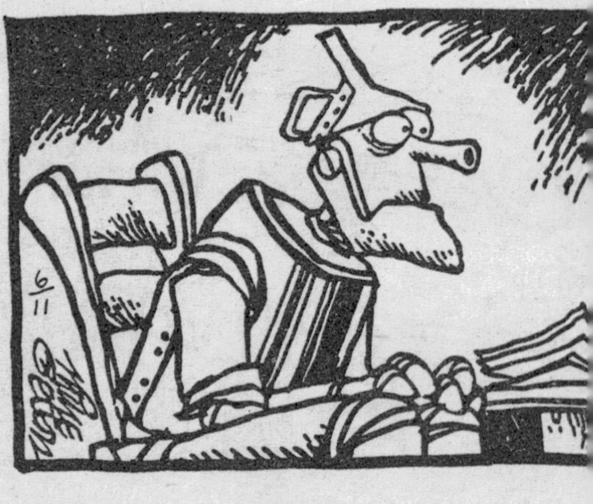
6/11

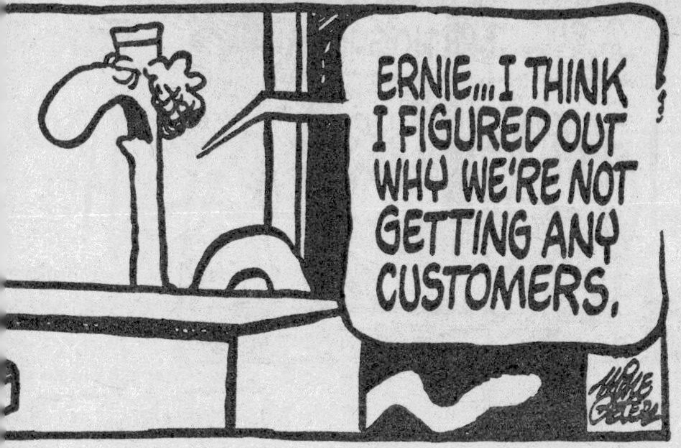
ERNIE...I THINK I FIGURED OUT WHY WE'RE NOT GETTING ANY CUSTOMERS.

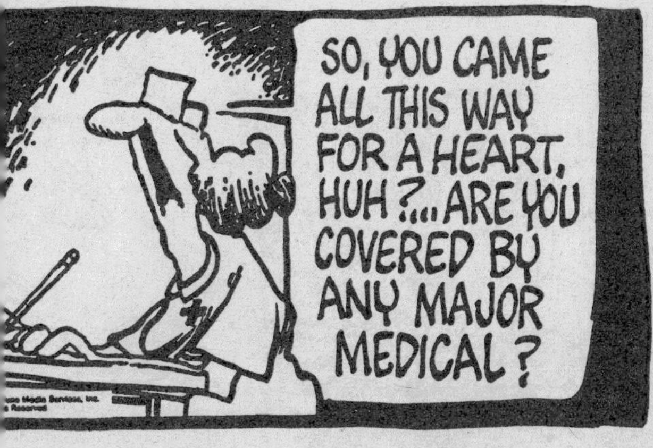
SO, YOU CAME ALL THIS WAY FOR A HEART, HUH ?...ARE YOU COVERED BY ANY MAJOR MEDICAL ?

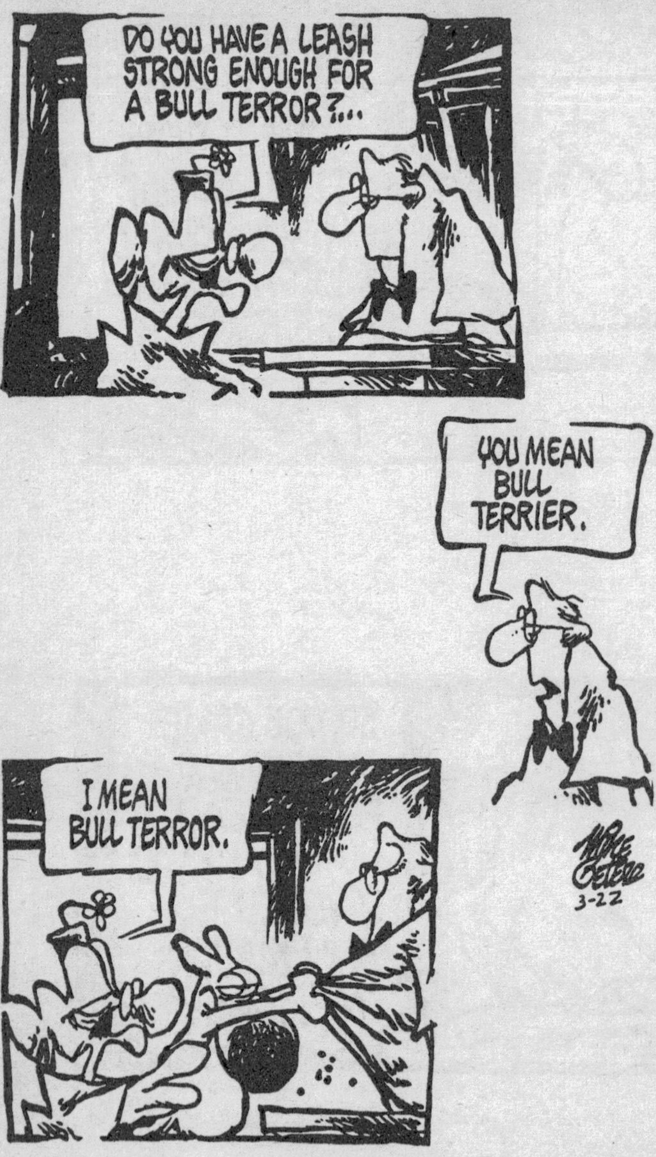
DO YOU HAVE A LEASH STRONG ENOUGH FOR A BULL TERROR?...
YOU MEAN BULL TERRIER.
I MEAN BULL TERROR.
3-22

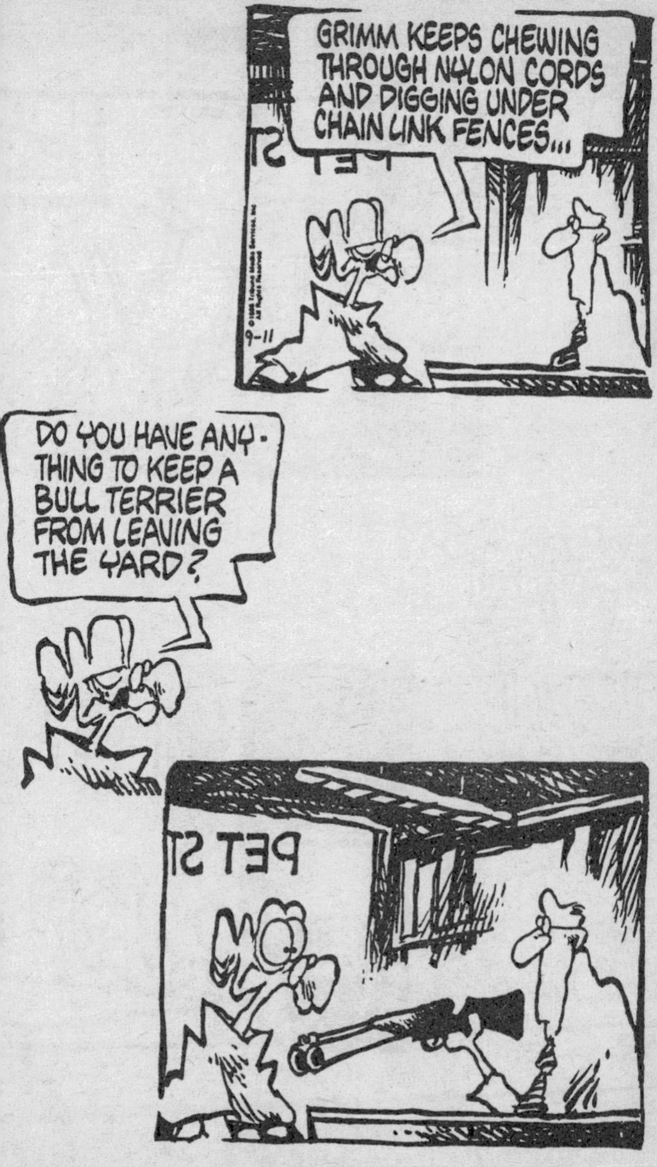
GRIMM KEEPS CHEWING THROUGH NYLON CORDS AND DIGGING UNDER CHAIN LINK FENCES...
9-11
DO YOU HAVE ANY-THING TO KEEP A BULL TERRIER FROM LEAVING THE YARD?

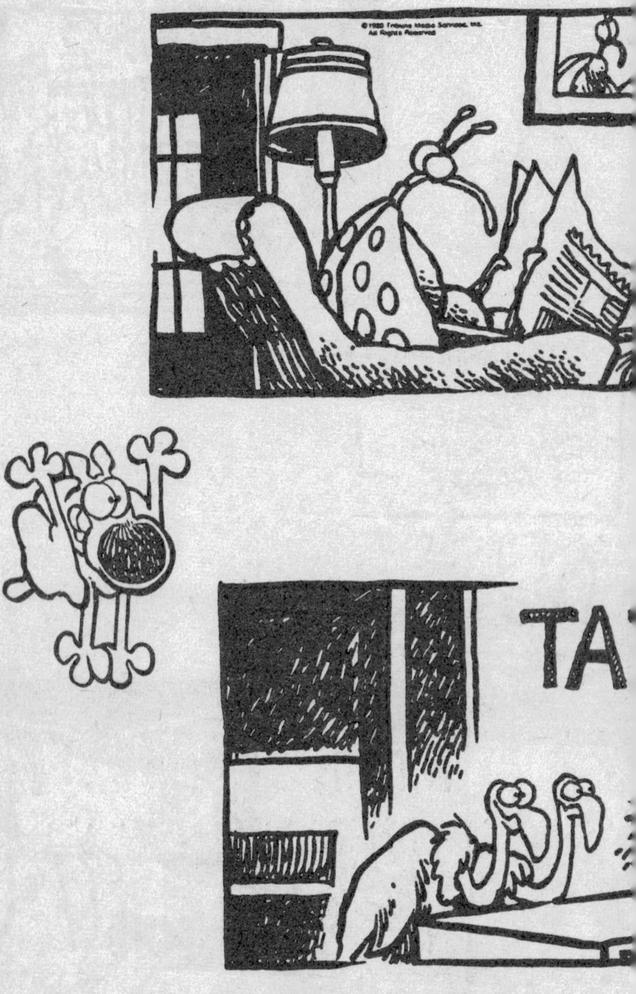
TA

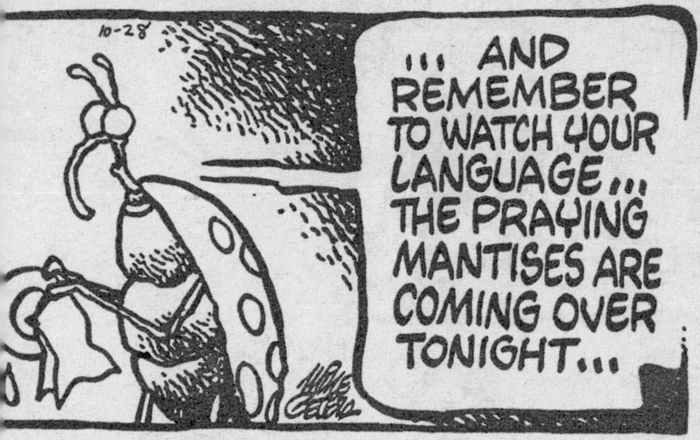
10-28
... AND REMEMBER TO WATCH YOUR LANGUAGE... THE PRAYING MANTISES ARE COMING OVER TONIGHT...

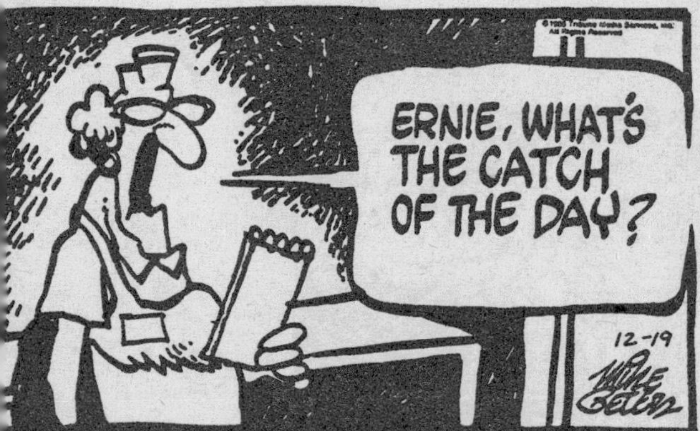
ERNIE, WHAT'S THE CATCH OF THE DAY?
12-19

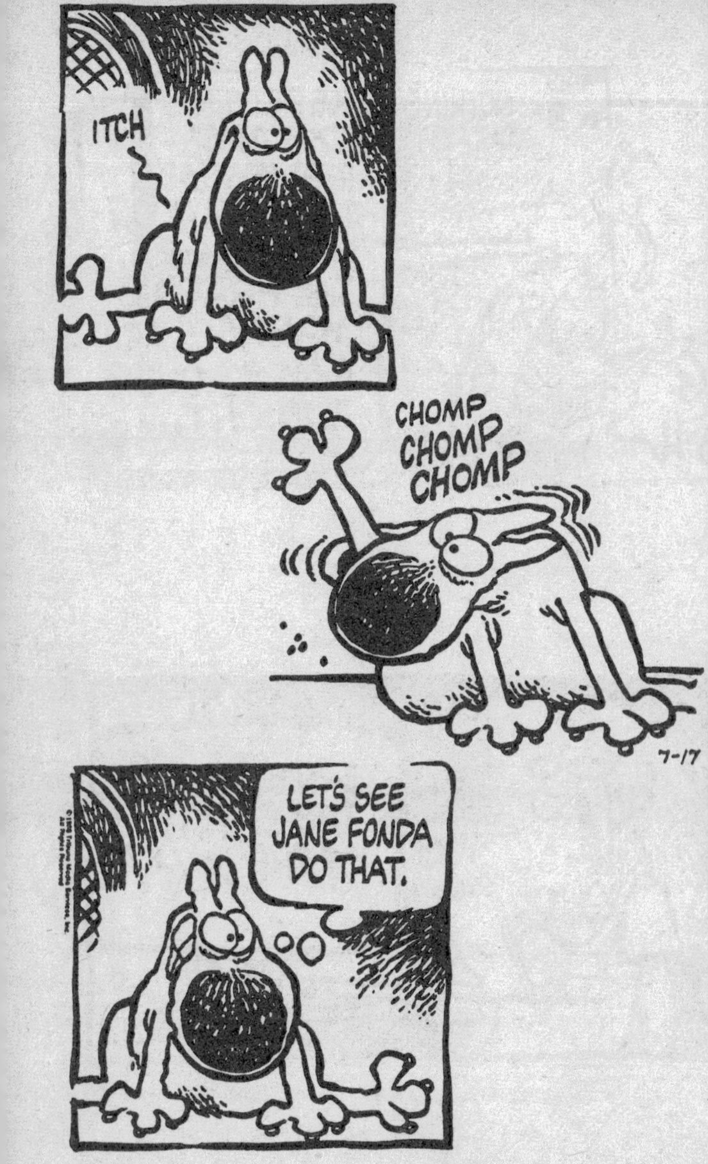
ITCH
CHOMP
CHOMP
CHOMP
7-17
LET'S SEE JANE FONDA DO THAT.

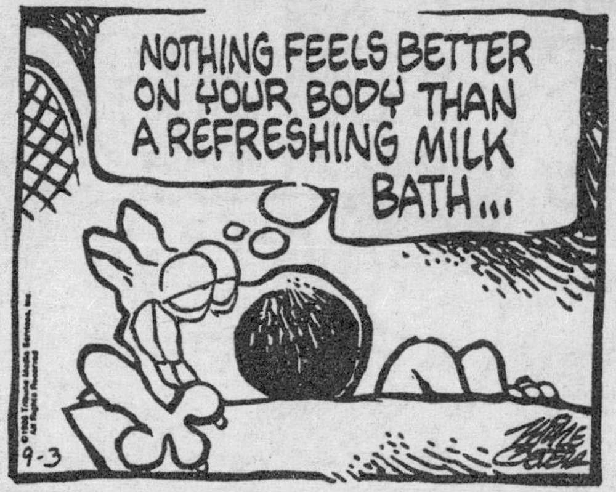
NOTHING FEELS BETTER ON YOUR BODY THAN A REFRESHING MILK BATH...
9-3

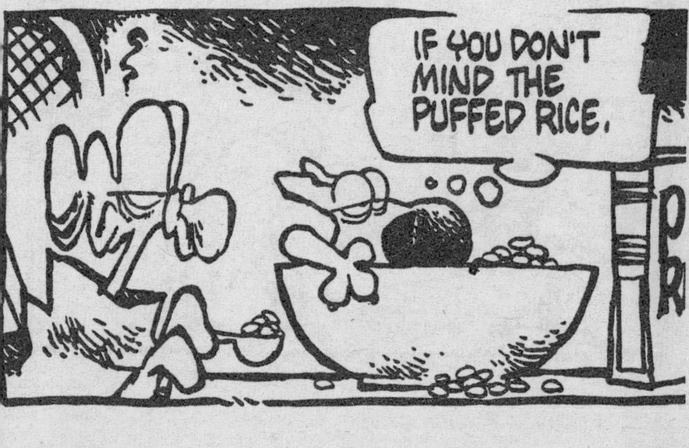
IF YOU DON'T MIND THE PUFFED RICE.

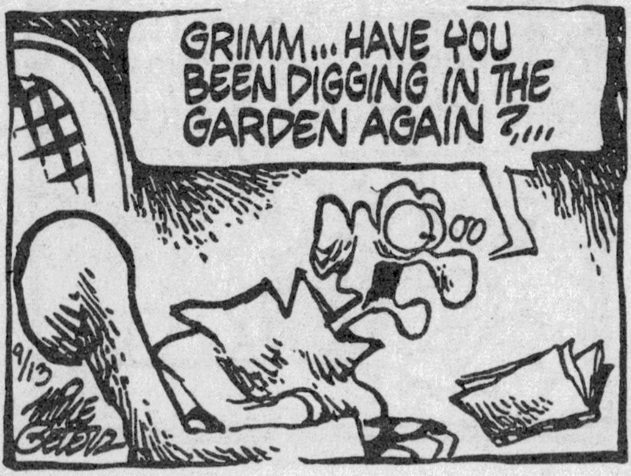
GRIMM... HAVE YOU BEEN DIGGING IN THE GARDEN AGAIN?....

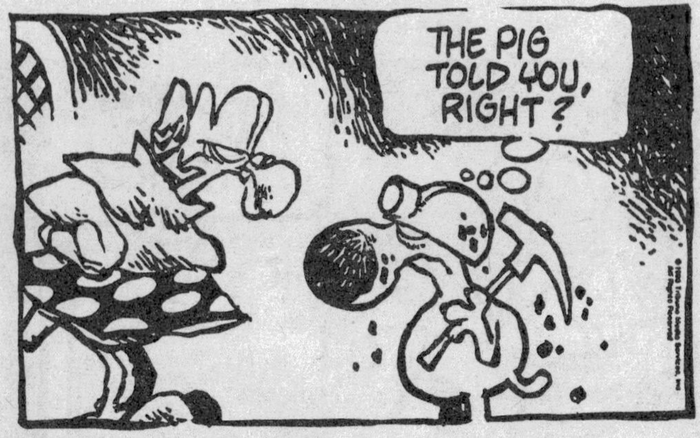
THE PIG TOLD YOU, RIGHT?

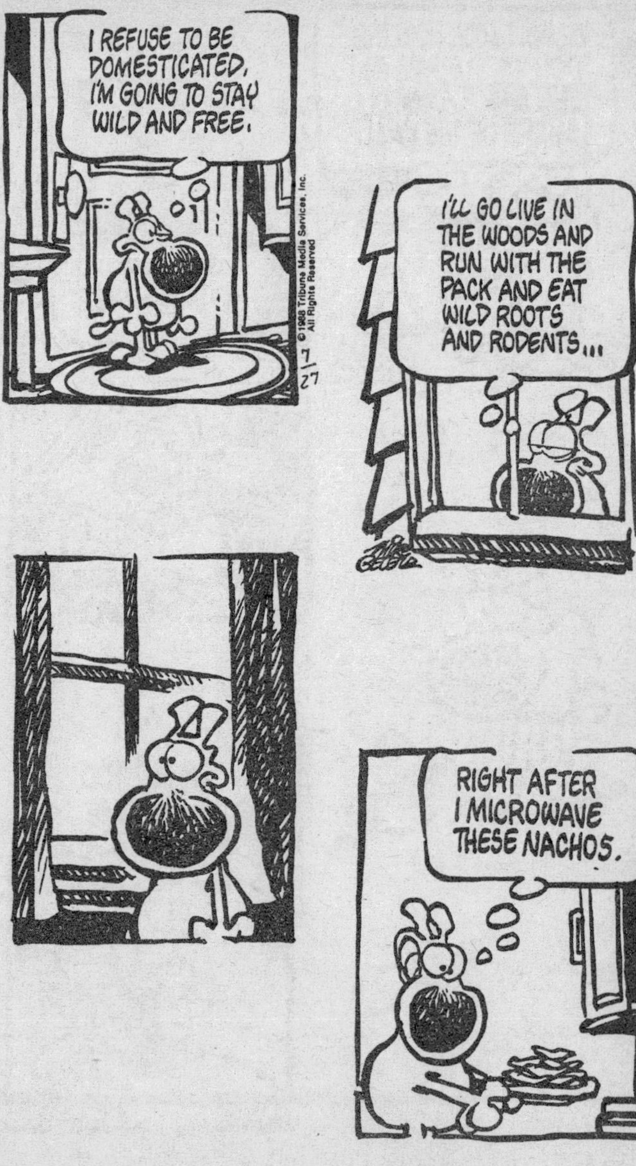
I REFUSE TO BE DOMESTICATED. I'M GOING TO STAY WILD AND FREE.
© 1988 Tribune Media Services, Inc. All Rights Reserved
7/27
I'LL GO LIVE IN THE WOODS AND RUN WITH THE PACK AND EAT WILD ROOTS AND RODENTS...
RIGHT AFTER I MICROWAVE THESE NACHOS.

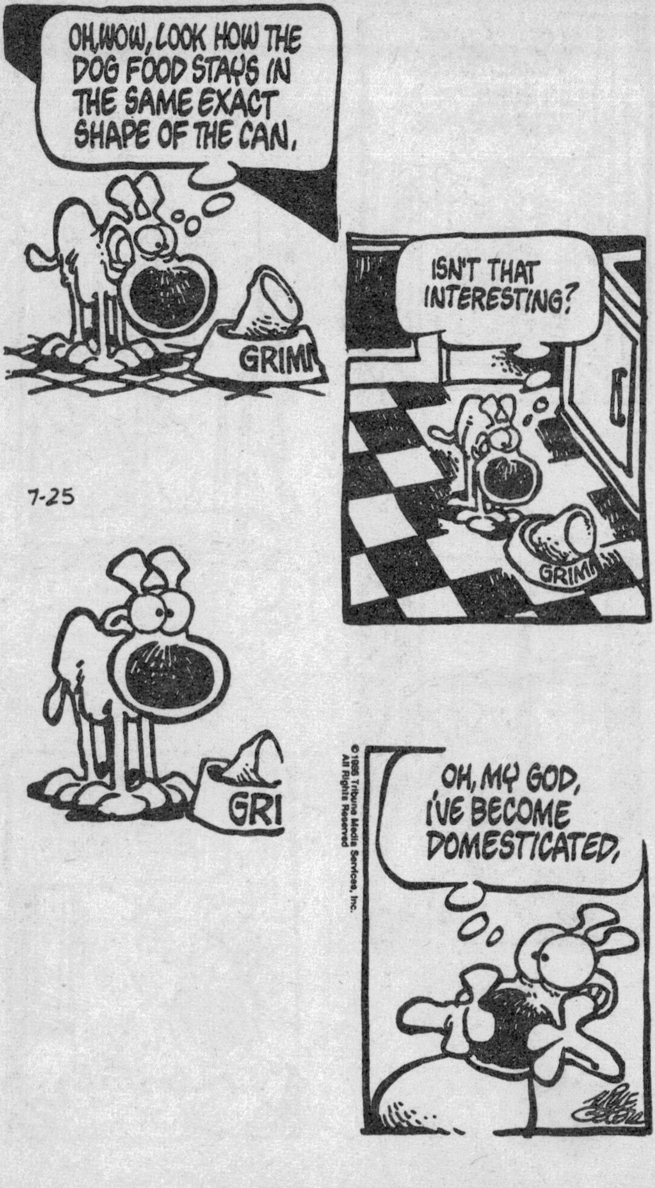
OH, WOW, LOOK HOW THE DOG FOOD STAYS IN THE SAME EXACT SHAPE OF THE CAN.
GRIMM
ISN'T THAT INTERESTING?
GRIMM
7-25
GRI
OH, MY GOD, I'VE BECOME DOMESTICATED.
© 1988 Tribune Media Services, Inc.
All Rights Reserved

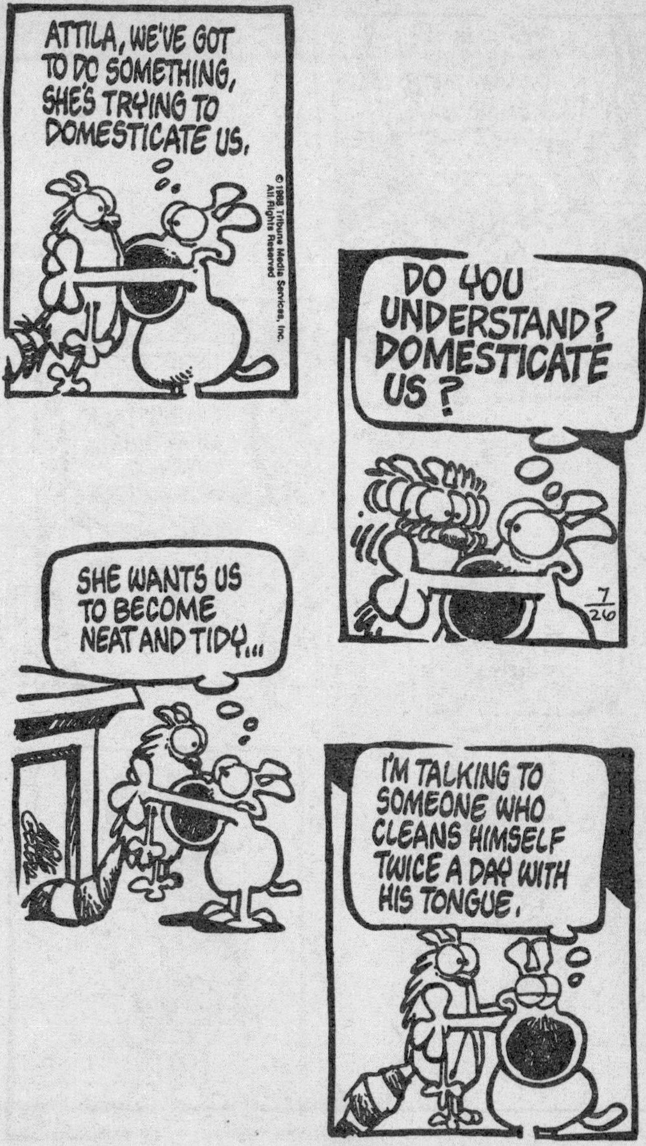
ATTILA, WE'VE GOT TO DO SOMETHING, SHE'S TRYING TO DOMESTICATE US.
© 1988 Tribune Media Services, Inc. All Rights Reserved
DO YOU UNDERSTAND? DOMESTICATE US?
7/26
SHE WANTS US TO BECOME NEAT AND TIDY...
I'M TALKING TO SOMEONE WHO CLEANS HIMSELF TWICE A DAY WITH HIS TONGUE.

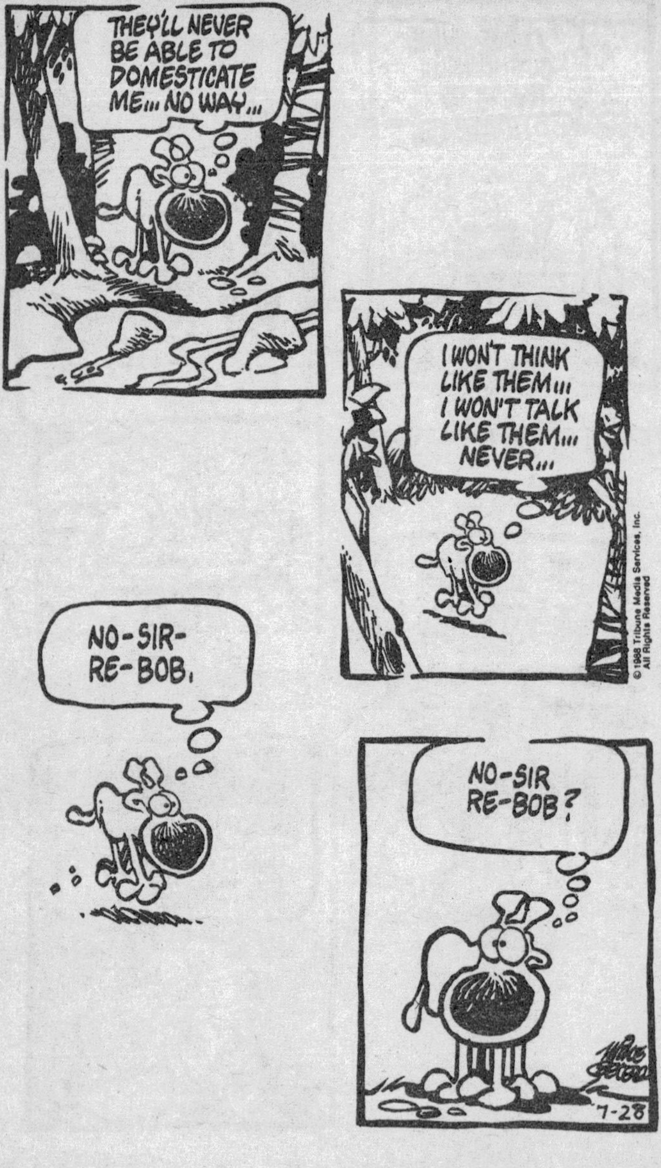
THEY'LL NEVER BE ABLE TO DOMESTICATE ME... NO WAY...
I WON'T THINK LIKE THEM... I WON'T TALK LIKE THEM... NEVER...
NO-SIR-RE-BOB.
NO-SIR RE-BOB?
7-28

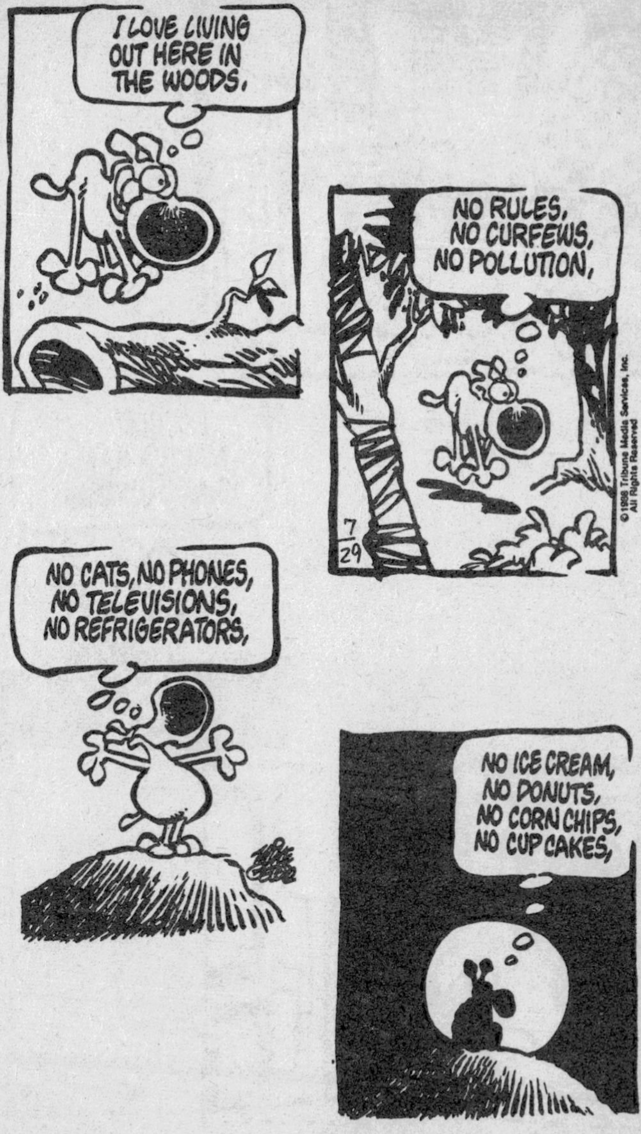
I LOVE LIVING OUT HERE IN THE WOODS.
NO RULES, NO CURFEWS, NO POLLUTION,
7/29
NO CATS, NO PHONES, NO TELEVISIONS, NO REFRIGERATORS,
NO ICE CREAM, NO DONUTS, NO CORN CHIPS, NO CUP CAKES,

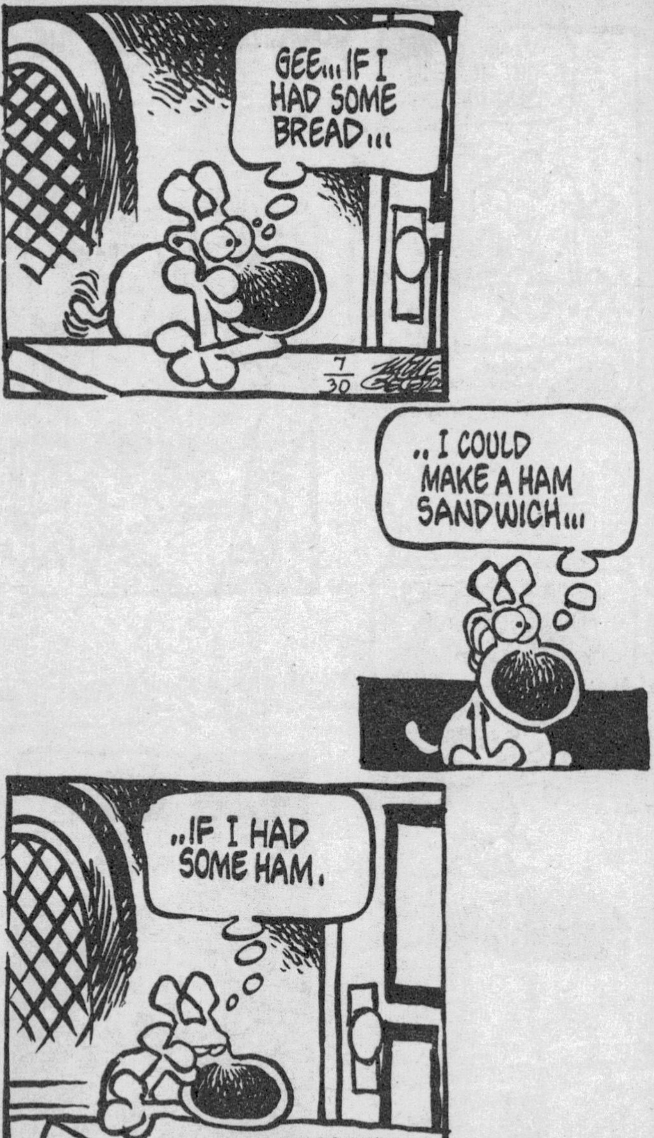
GEE... IF I HAD SOME BREAD...
7/30
.. I COULD MAKE A HAM SANDWICH...
..IF I HAD SOME HAM.
© 1988 Tribune Media Services, Inc.
All Rights Reserved

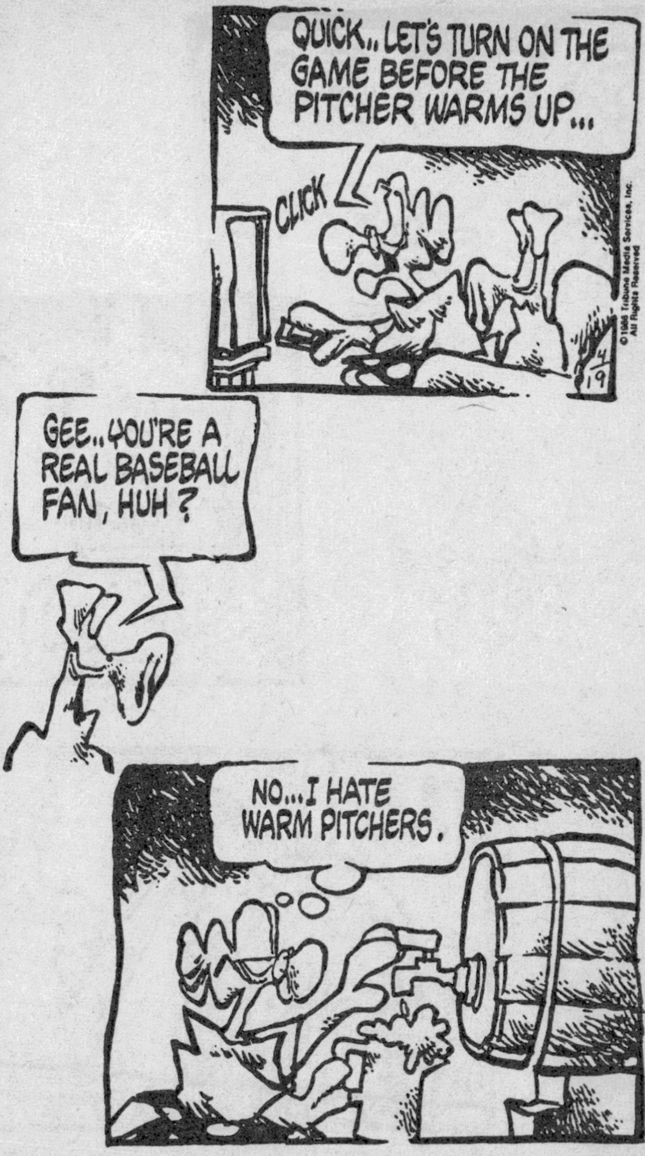
QUICK.. LET'S TURN ON THE GAME BEFORE THE PITCHER WARMS UP...
CLICK
GEE.. YOU'RE A REAL BASEBALL FAN, HUH?
NO...I HATE WARM PITCHERS.

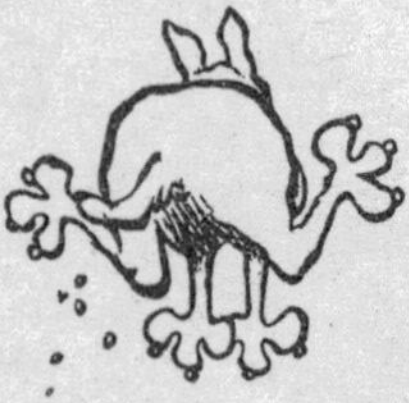

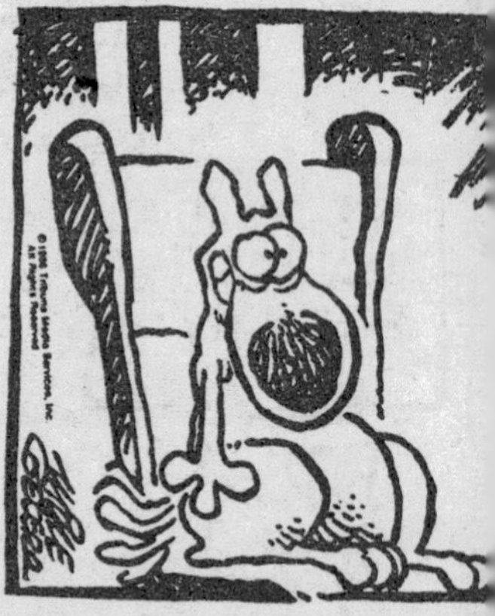

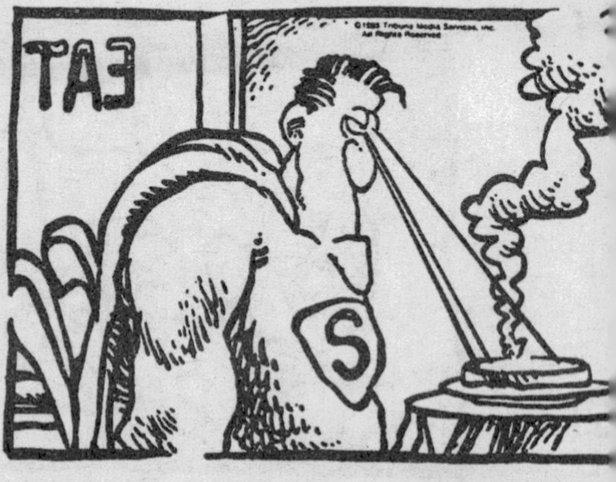
Tribune Media Services, Inc.
All Rights Reserved

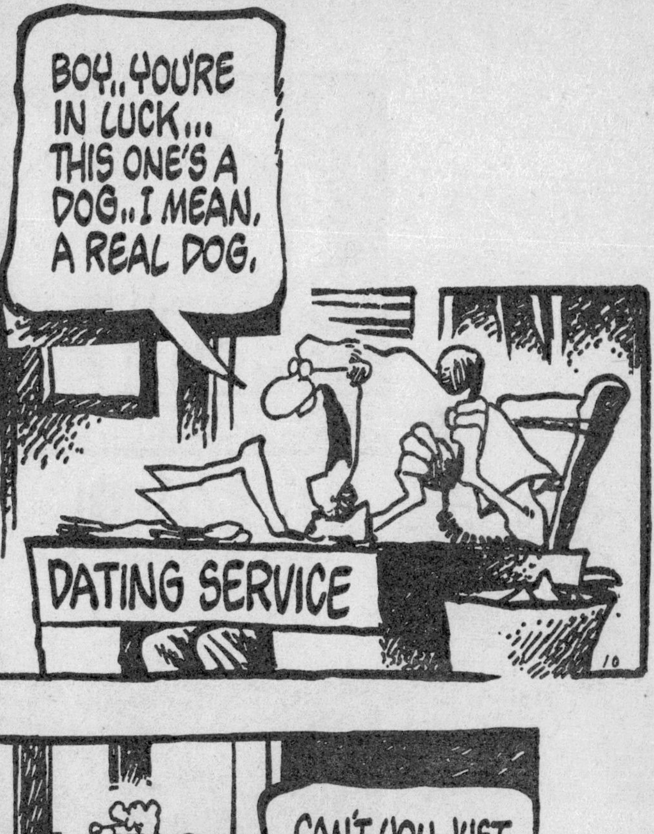
BOY.. YOU'RE IN LUCK... THIS ONE'S A DOG.. I MEAN, A REAL DOG.
DATING SERVICE

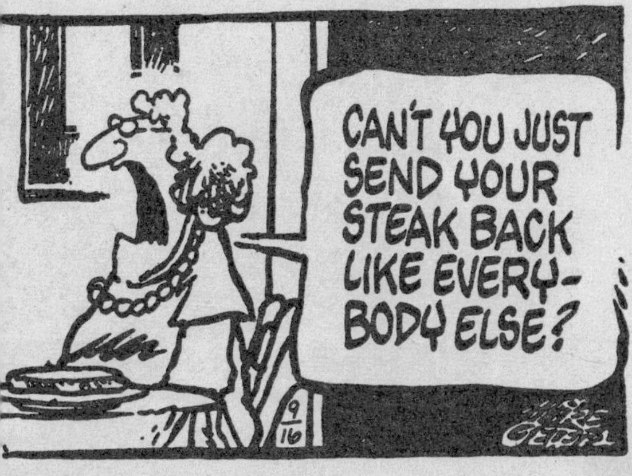
CAN'T YOU JUST SEND YOUR STEAK BACK LIKE EVERY-BODY ELSE?

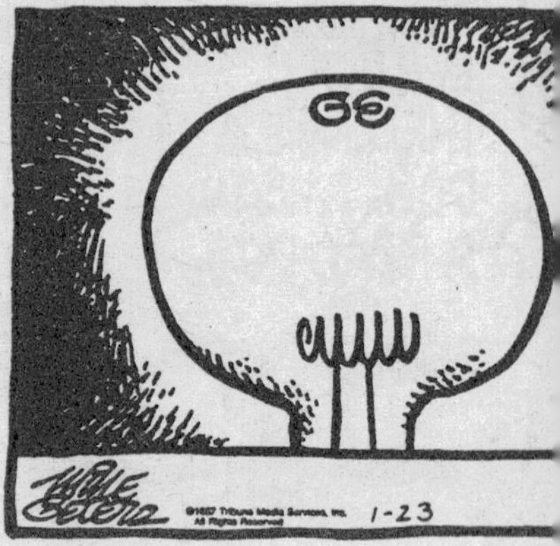
©1987 Tribune Media Services, Inc.
All Rights Reserved
1-23

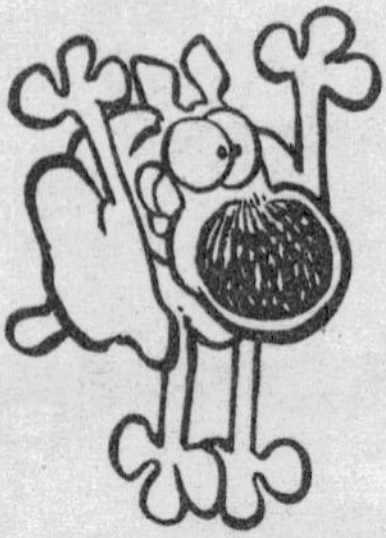

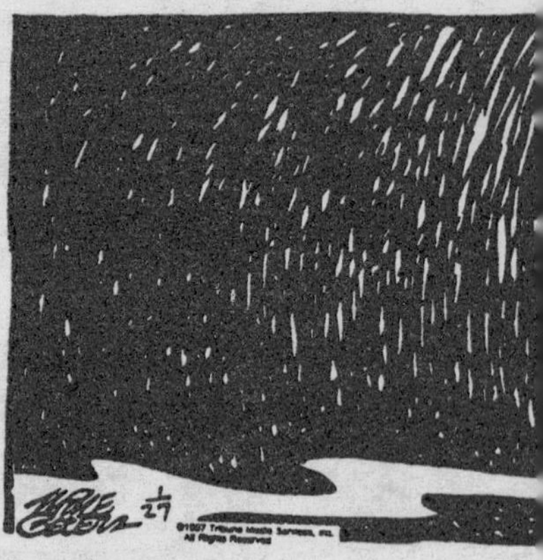
1/27
©1987 Tribune Media Services, Inc.
All Rights Reserved

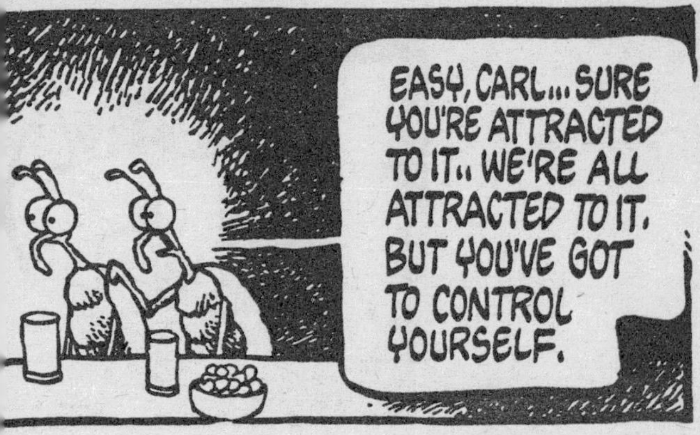
EASY, CARL... SURE YOU'RE ATTRACTED TO IT.. WE'RE ALL ATTRACTED TO IT. BUT YOU'VE GOT TO CONTROL YOURSELF.

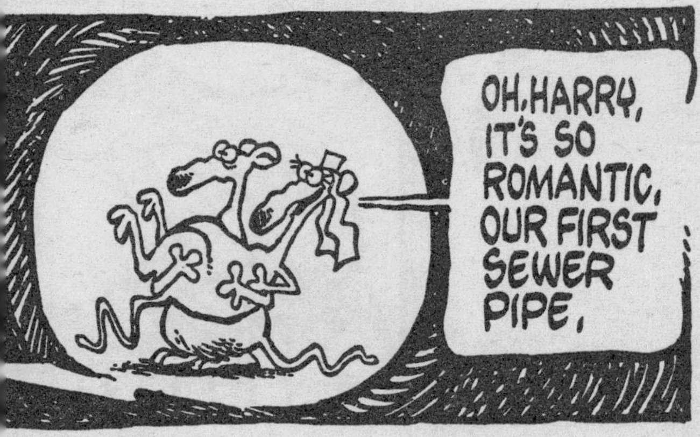
OH, HARRY, IT'S SO ROMANTIC, OUR FIRST SEWER PIPE.

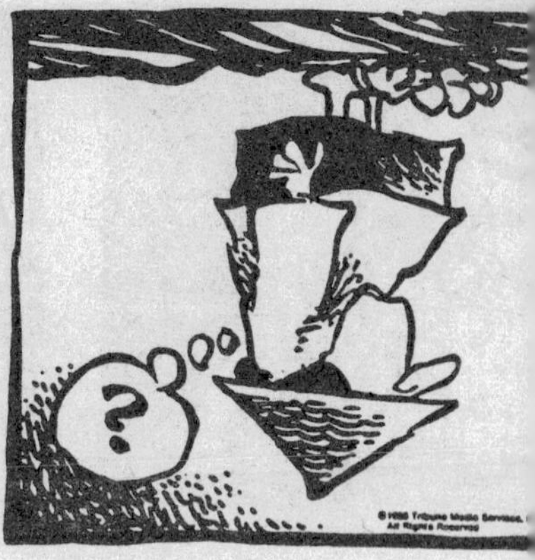
?

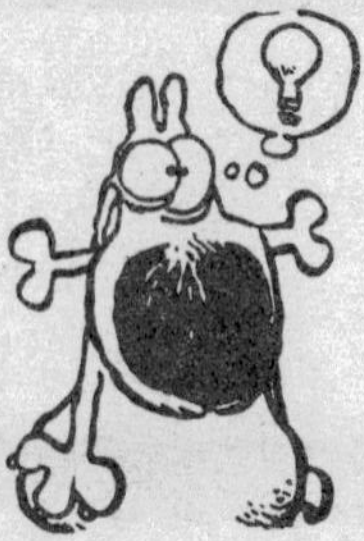

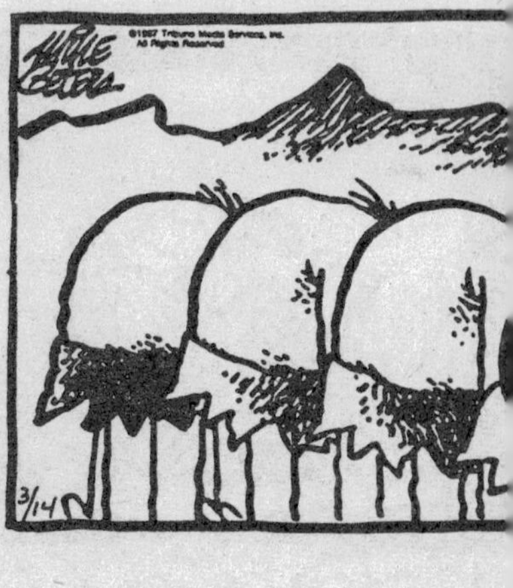
©1987 Tribune Media Services, Inc.
All Rights Reserved
3/14

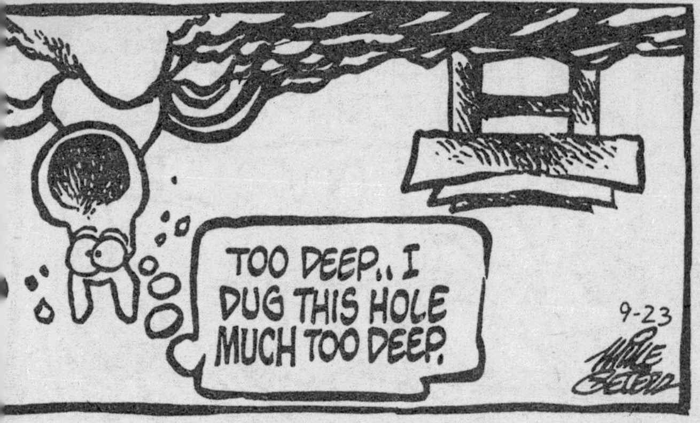
TOO DEEP.. I DUG THIS HOLE MUCH TOO DEEP.
9-23

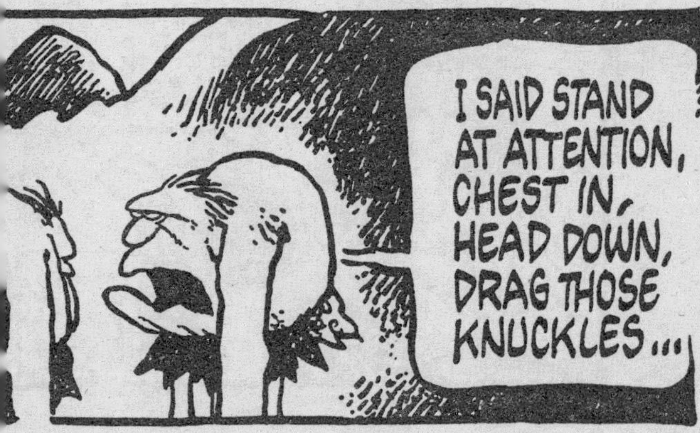
I SAID STAND AT ATTENTION, CHEST IN, HEAD DOWN, DRAG THOSE KNUCKLES...

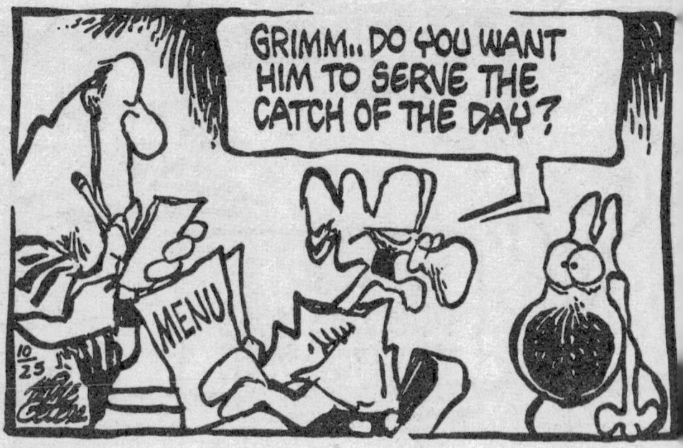
GRIMM.. DO YOU WANT HIM TO SERVE THE CATCH OF THE DAY?
MENU
10/25

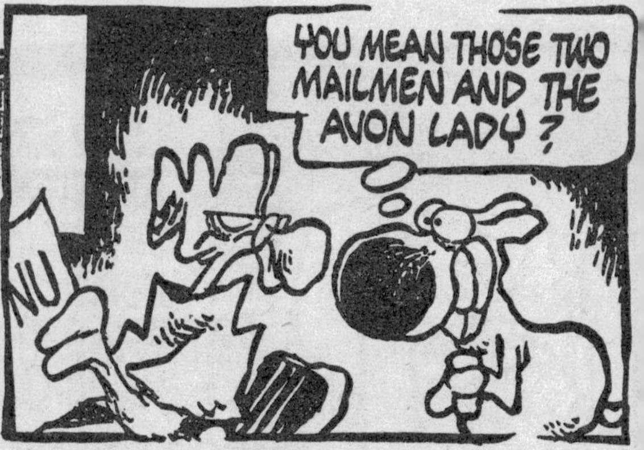
YOU MEAN THOSE TWO MAILMEN AND THE AVON LADY?
NU

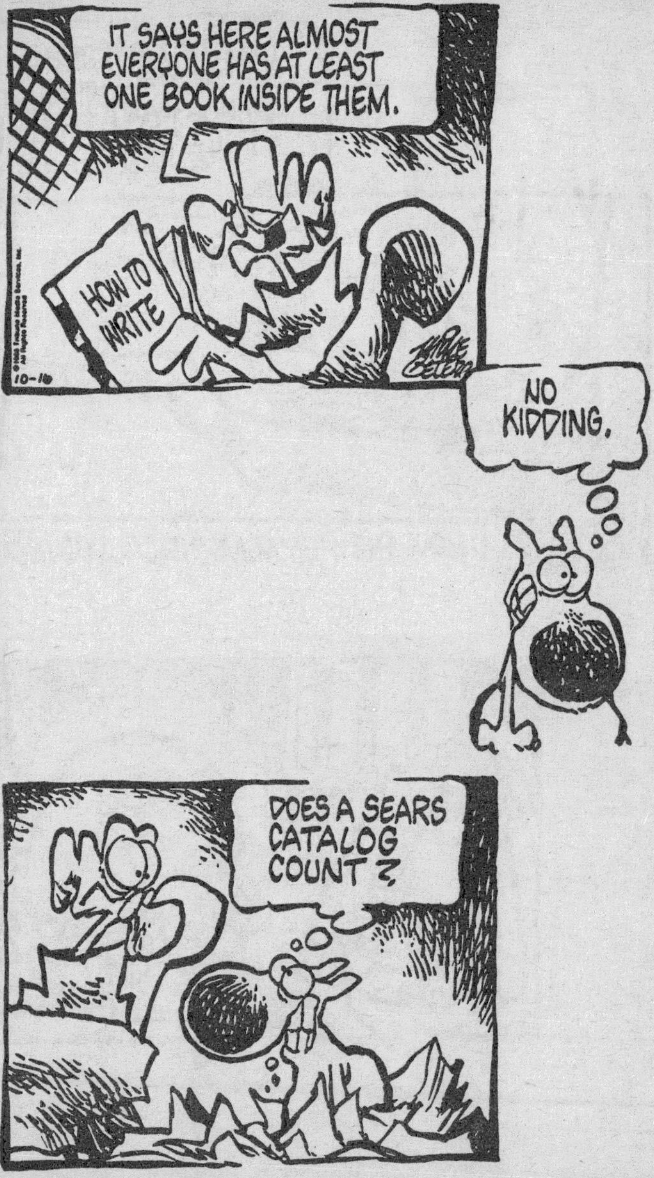
IT SAYS HERE ALMOST EVERYONE HAS AT LEAST ONE BOOK INSIDE THEM.
HOW TO WRITE
10-10
NO KIDDING.
DOES A SEARS CATALOG COUNT?

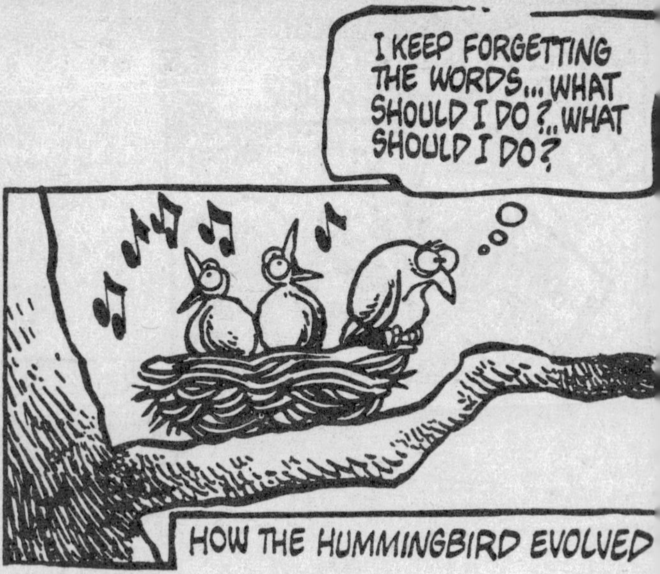
I KEEP FORGETTING THE WORDS... WHAT SHOULD I DO?... WHAT SHOULD I DO?
HOW THE HUMMINGBIRD EVOLVED

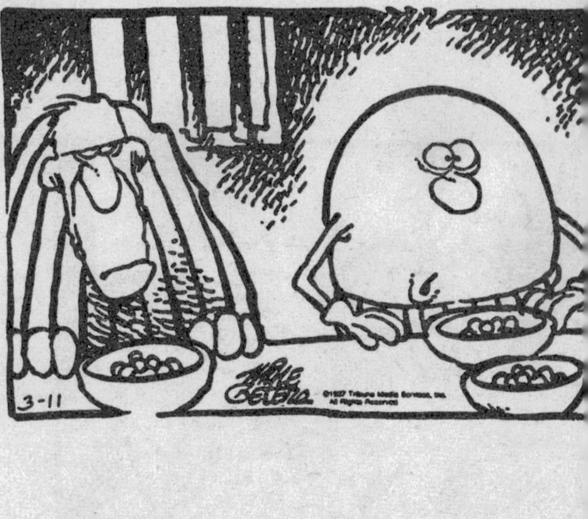
3-11

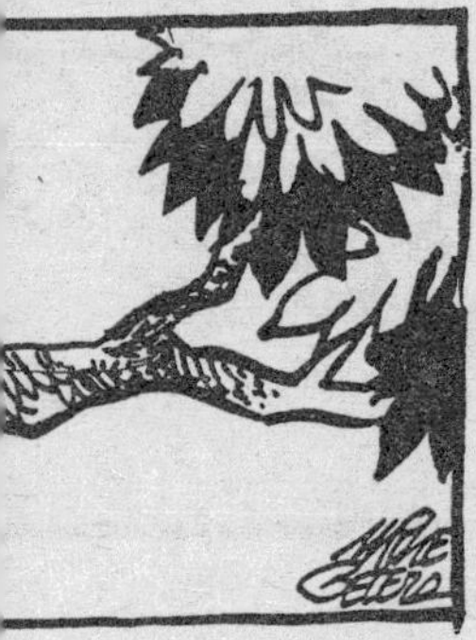

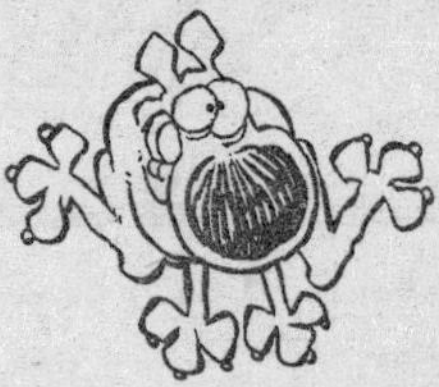

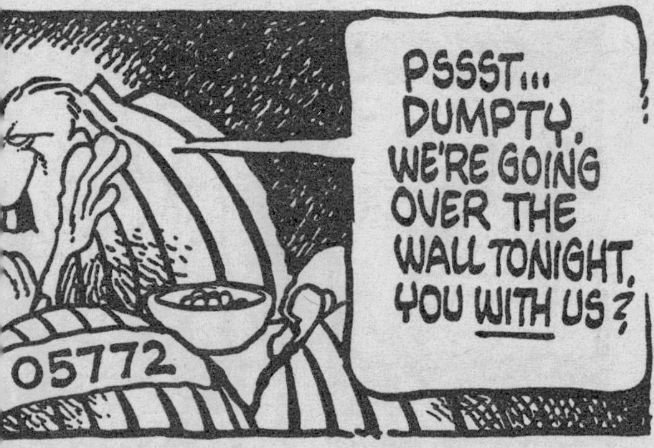
PSSST... DUMPTY, WE'RE GOING OVER THE WALL TONIGHT. YOU WITH US?
05772

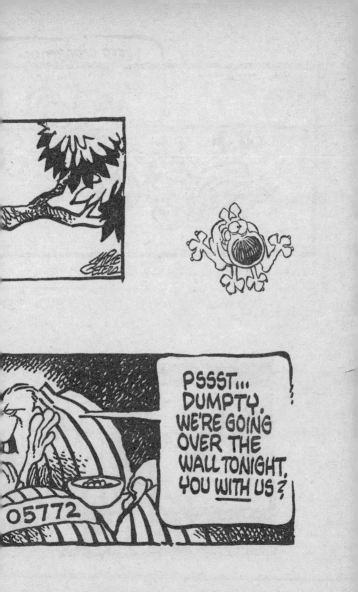

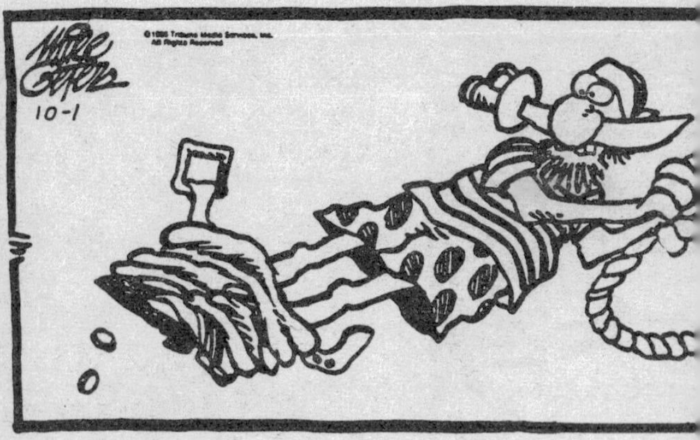
10-1

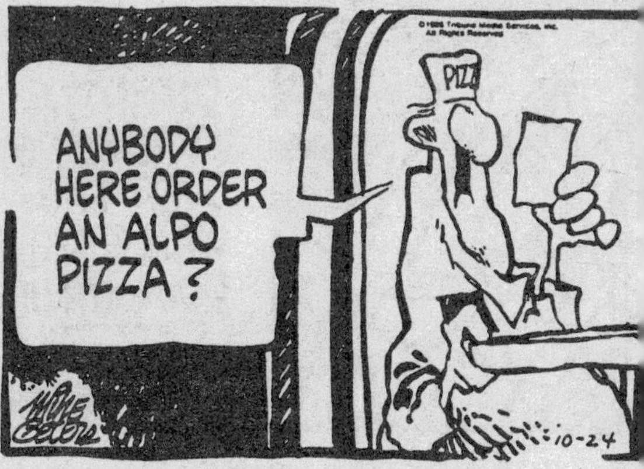
ANYBODY HERE ORDER AN ALPO PIZZA?
10-24

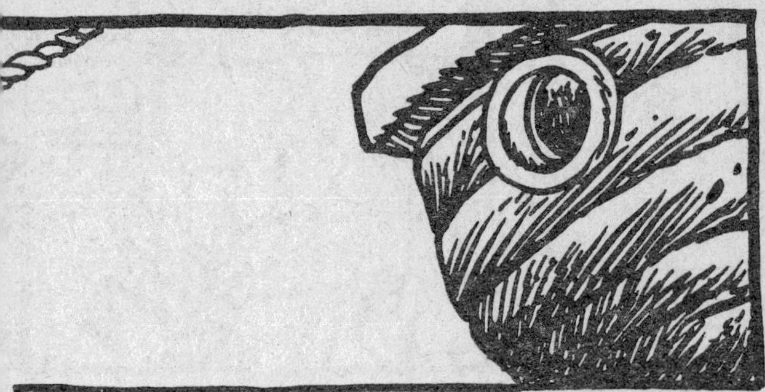

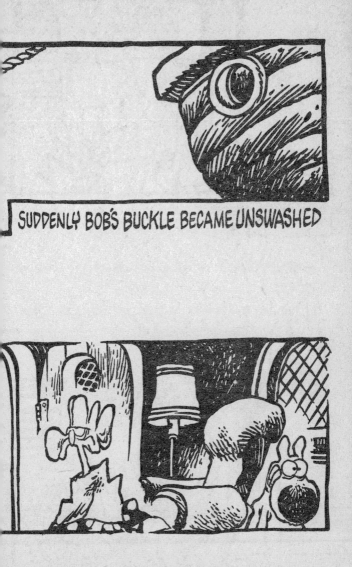

SUDDENLY BOB'S BUCKLE BECAME UNSWASHED

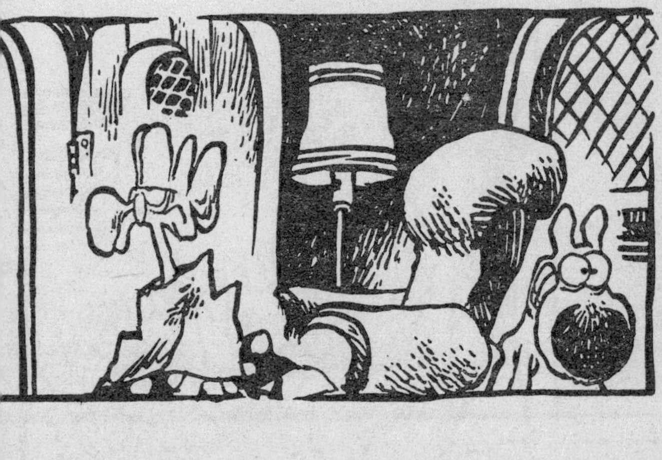

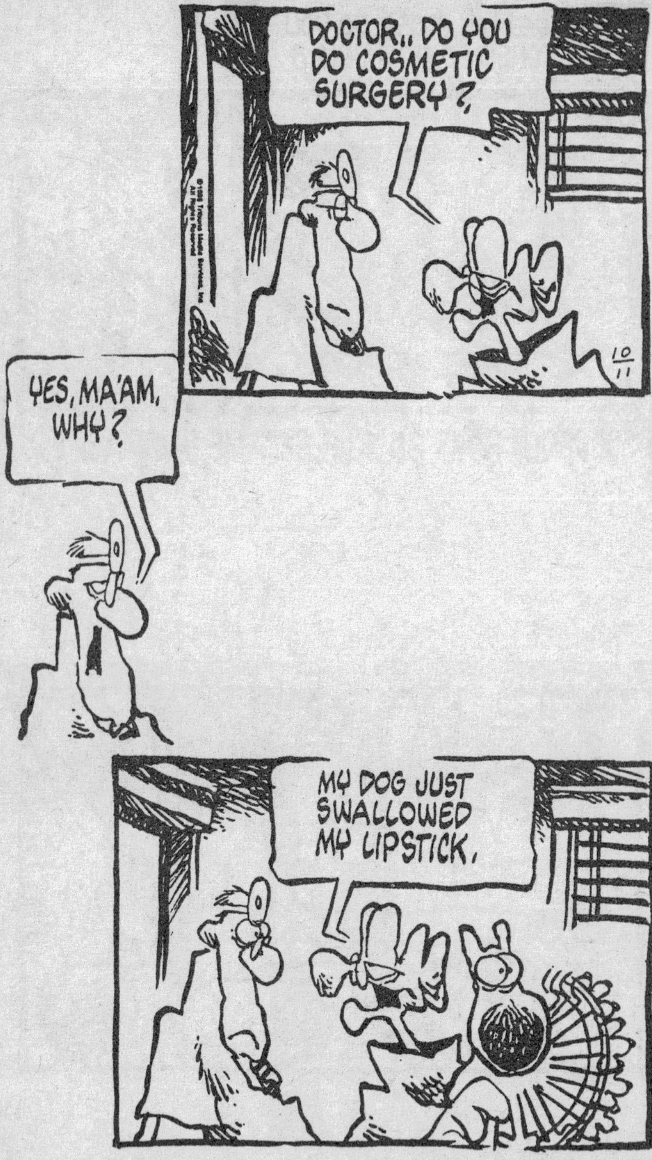
DOCTOR.. DO YOU DO COSMETIC SURGERY?
10/11
YES, MA'AM, WHY?
MY DOG JUST SWALLOWED MY LIPSTICK.

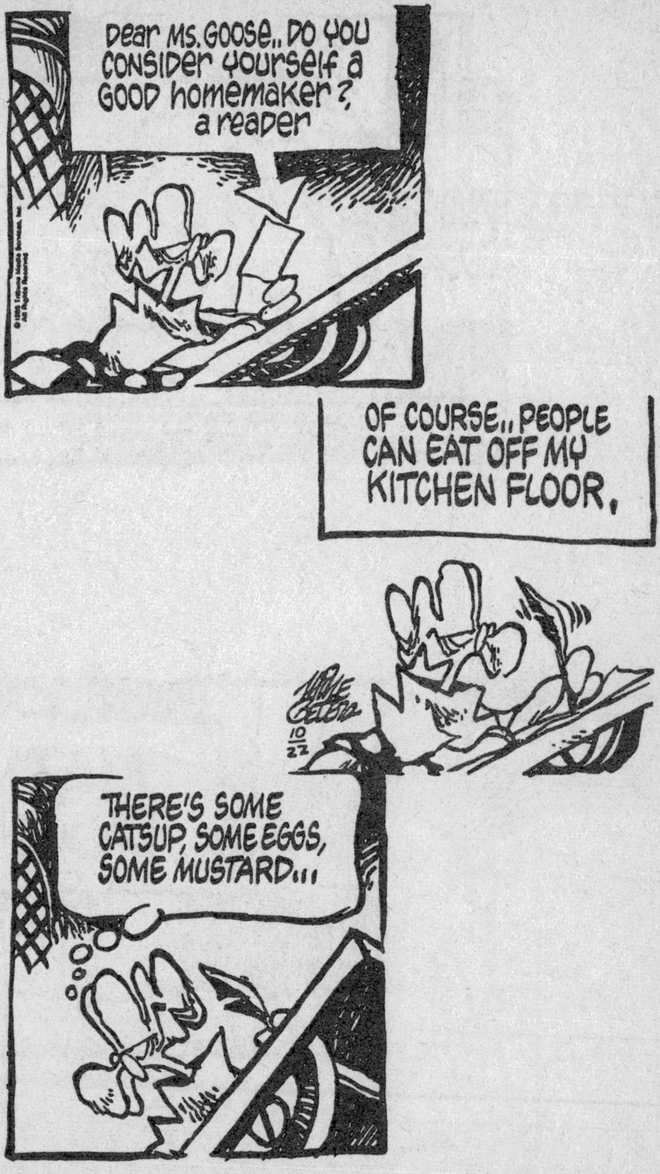
Dear MS. GOOSE.. DO YOU CONSIDER YOURSELF A GOOD homemaker? a reader
OF COURSE.. PEOPLE CAN EAT OFF MY KITCHEN FLOOR.
THERE'S SOME CATSUP, SOME EGGS, SOME MUSTARD...
10 22

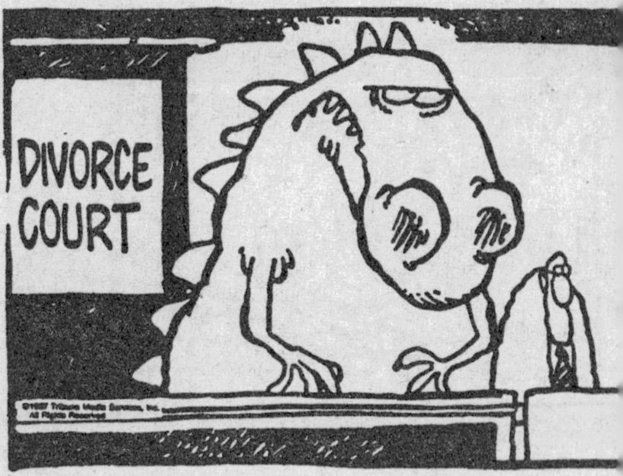
DIVORCE COURT

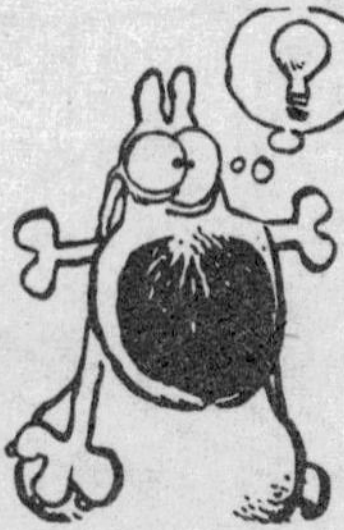

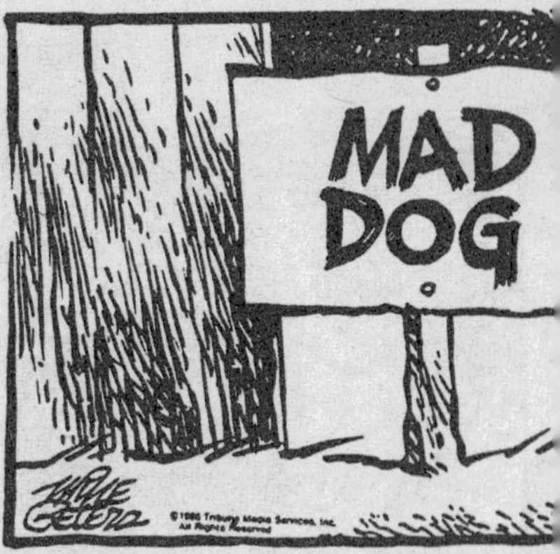
MAD DOG

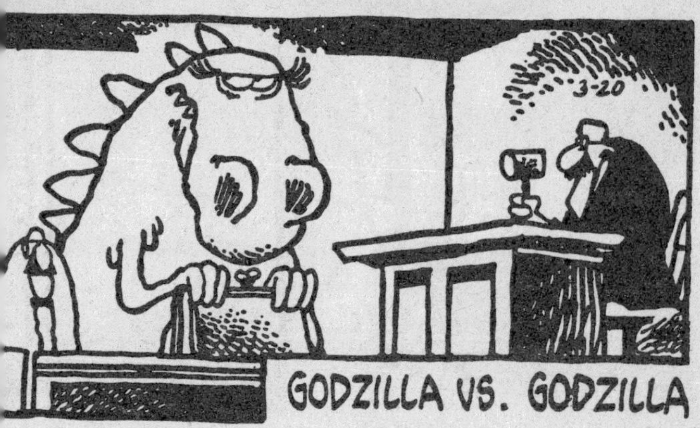
3-20
GODZILLA VS. GODZILLA

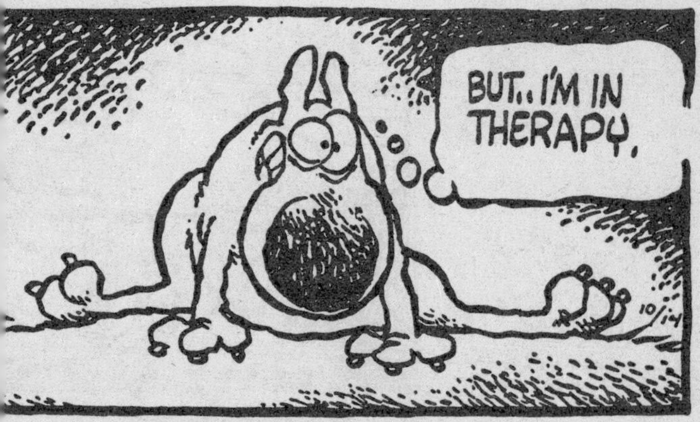
BUT.. I'M IN THERAPY.
10/14

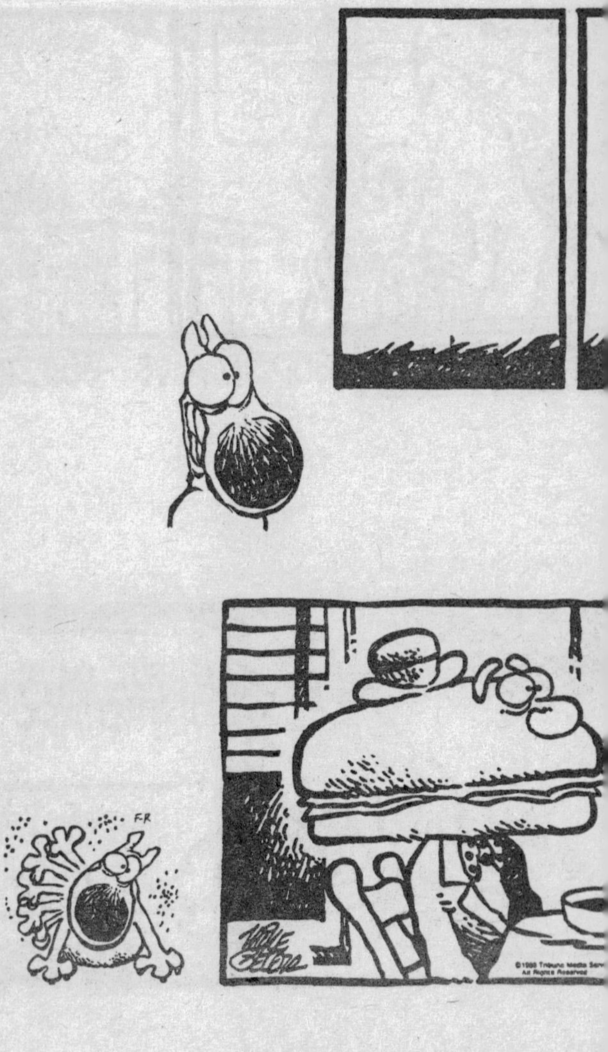
©1989 Tribune Media Serv
All Rights Reserved

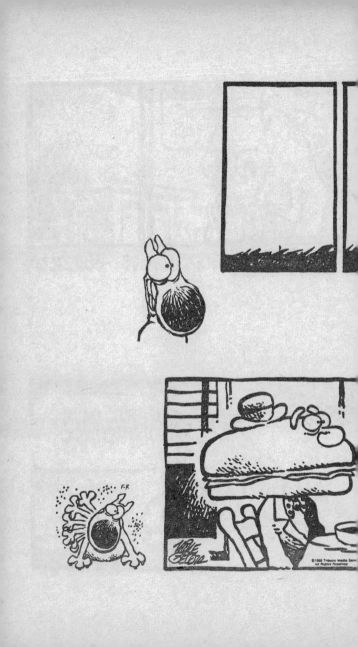

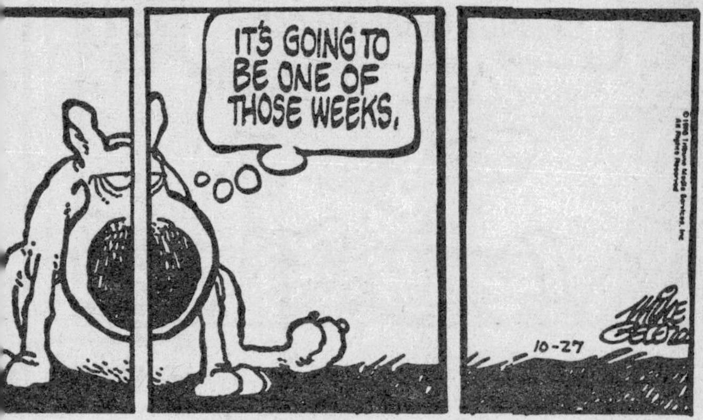
IT'S GOING TO BE ONE OF THOSE WEEKS.
10-27

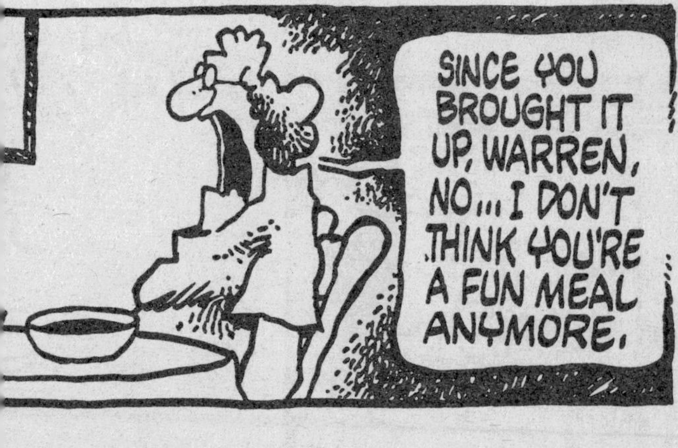
SINCE YOU BROUGHT IT UP, WARREN, NO... I DON'T THINK YOU'RE A FUN MEAL ANYMORE.

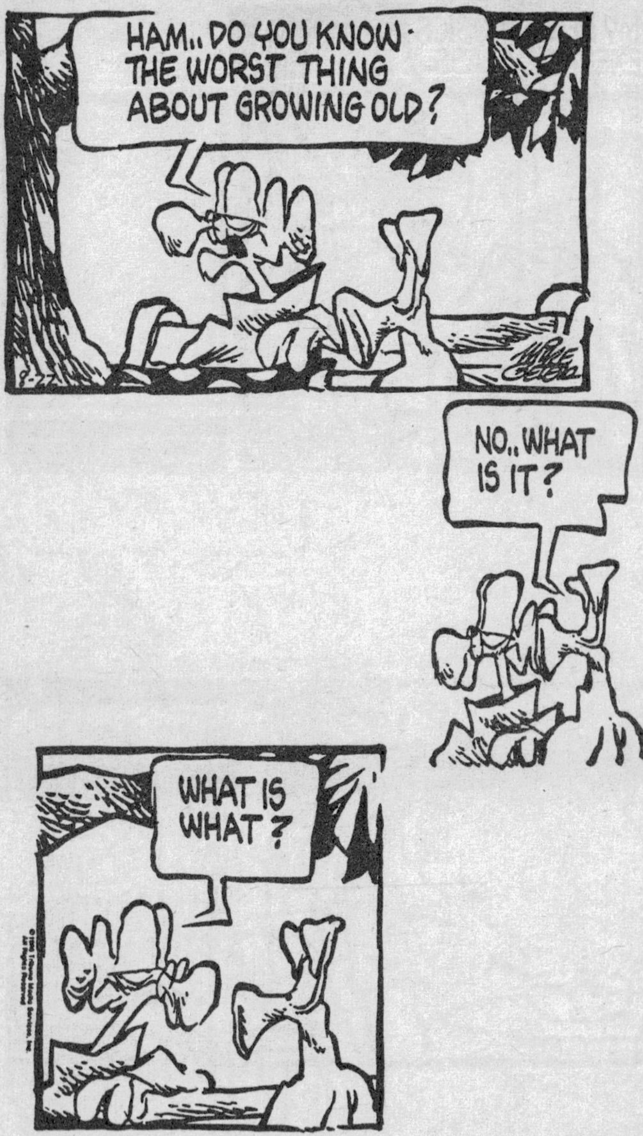
HAM.. DO YOU KNOW THE WORST THING ABOUT GROWING OLD?
NO.. WHAT IS IT?
WHAT IS WHAT?

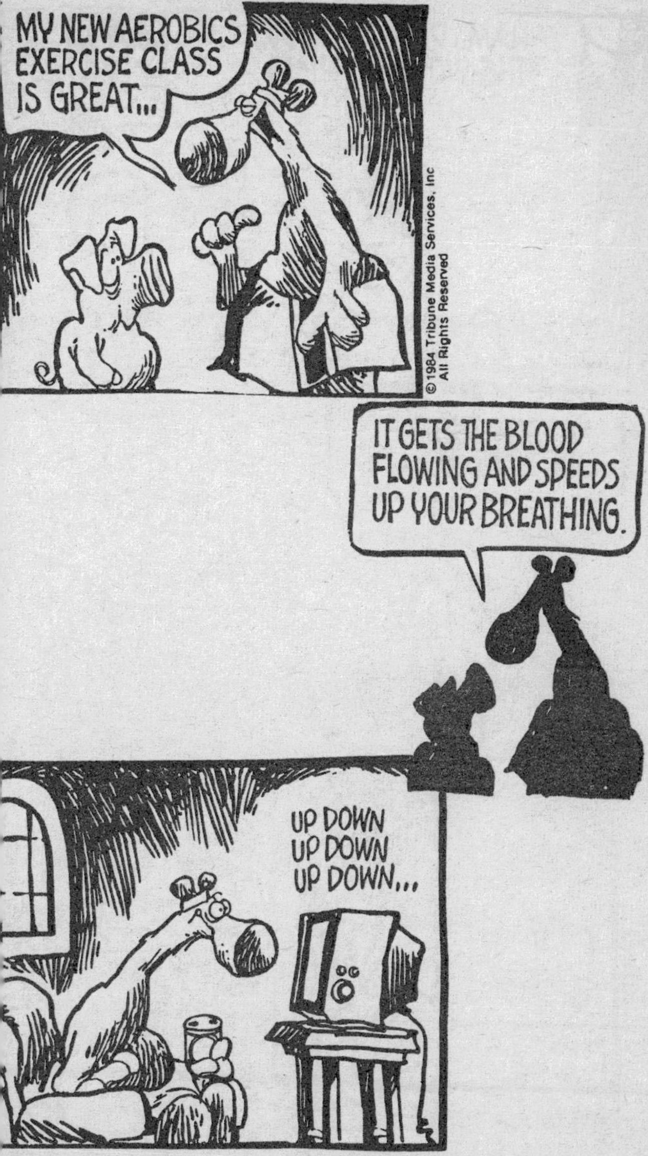
MY NEW AEROBICS EXERCISE CLASS IS GREAT...
IT GETS THE BLOOD FLOWING AND SPEEDS UP YOUR BREATHING.
UP DOWN UP DOWN UP DOWN...

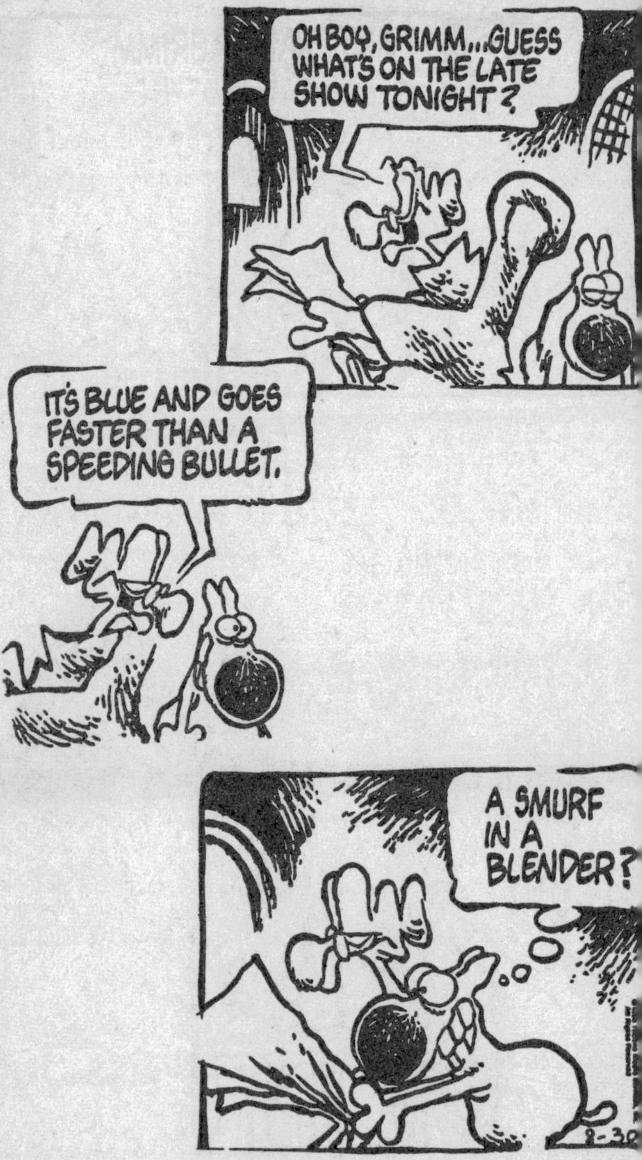
OH BOY, GRIMM...GUESS WHAT'S ON THE LATE SHOW TONIGHT?
IT'S BLUE AND GOES FASTER THAN A SPEEDING BULLET.
A SMURF IN A BLENDER?

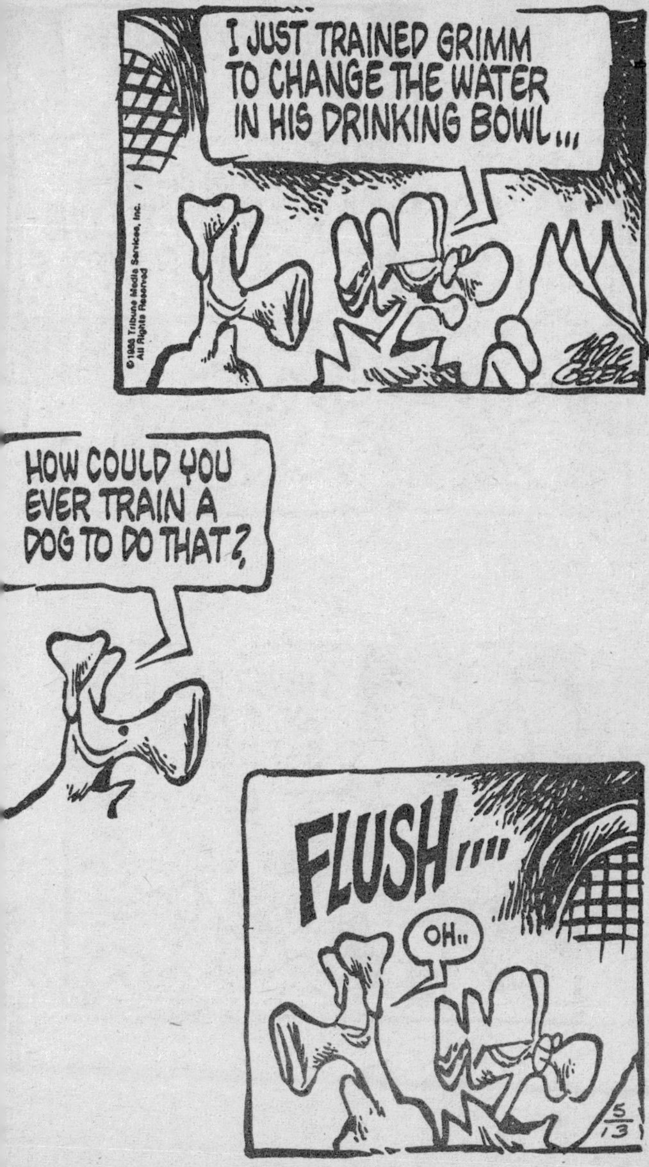
I JUST TRAINED GRIMM TO CHANGE THE WATER IN HIS DRINKING BOWL...
Tribune Media Services, Inc.
All Rights Reserved
HOW COULD YOU EVER TRAIN A DOG TO DO THAT?
FLUSH....
OH..
5/13

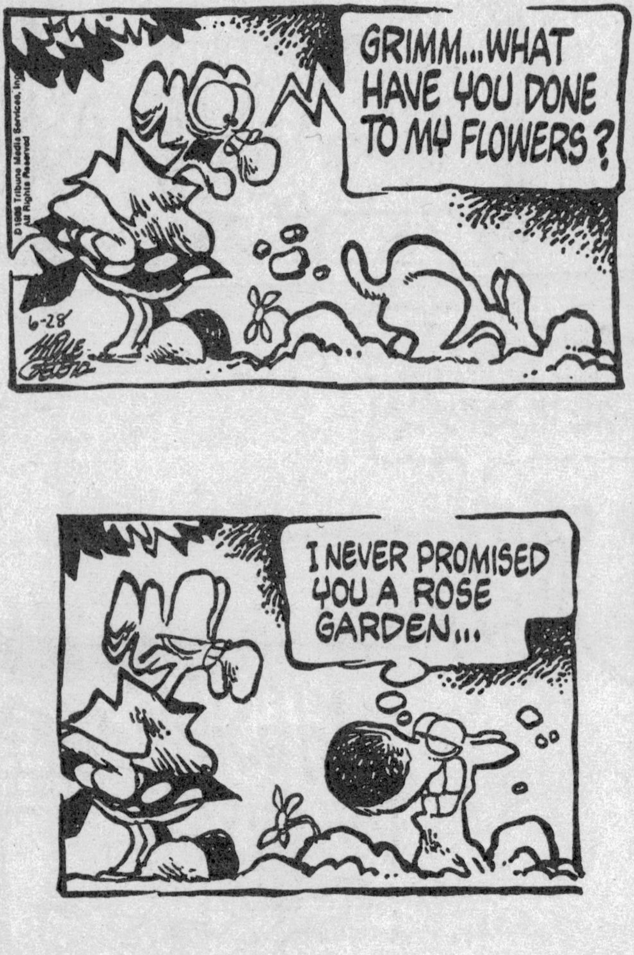
Tribune Media Services, Inc.
All Rights Reserved
6-28
GRIMM...WHAT HAVE YOU DONE TO MY FLOWERS?
I NEVER PROMISED YOU A ROSE GARDEN...

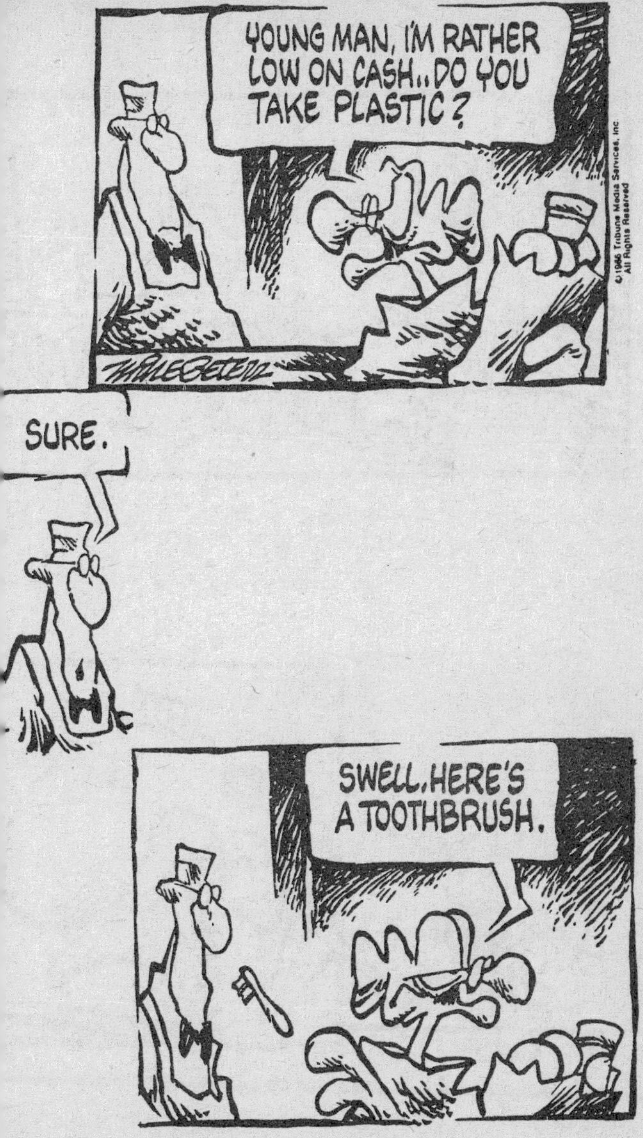
YOUNG MAN, I'M RATHER LOW ON CASH.. DO YOU TAKE PLASTIC?
SURE.
SWELL. HERE'S A TOOTHBRUSH.

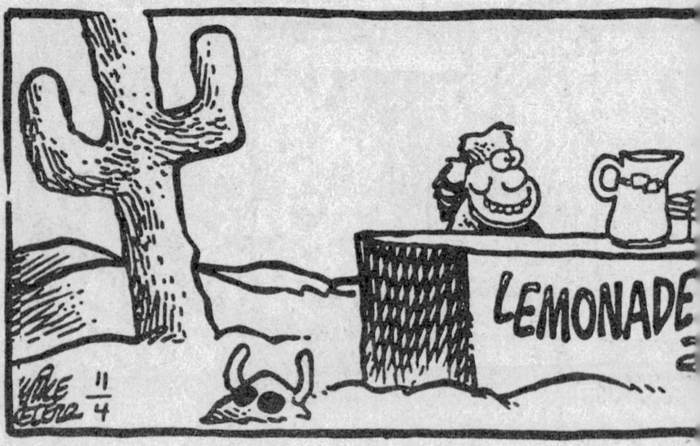
LEMONADE

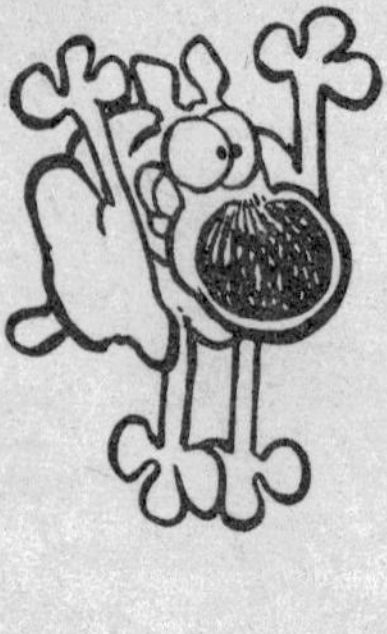

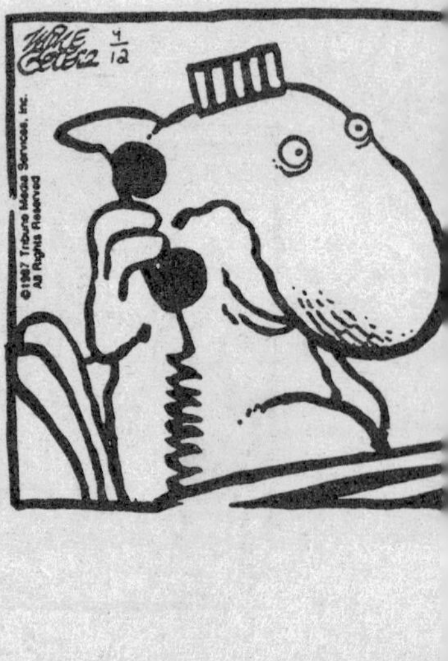
©1987 Tribune Media Services, Inc.
All Rights Reserved

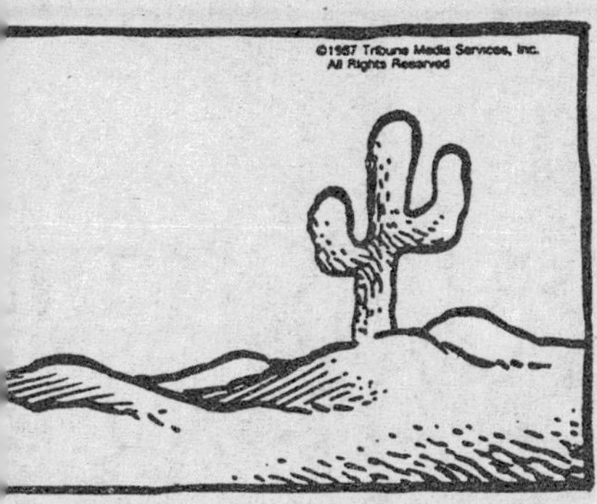
©1987 Tribune Media Services, Inc.
All Rights Reserved

CUSTER'S FIRST STAND

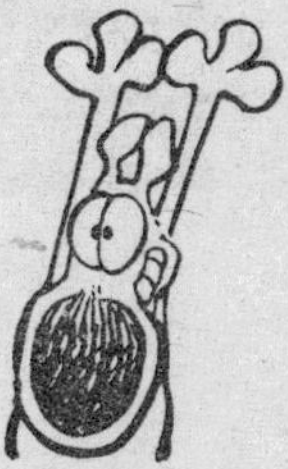

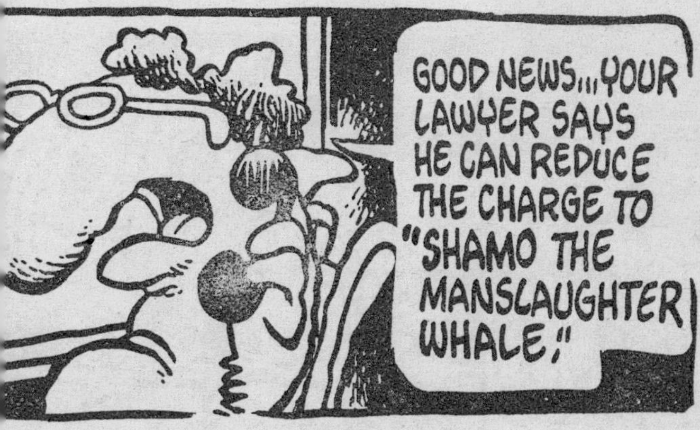
GOOD NEWS... YOUR LAWYER SAYS HE CAN REDUCE THE CHARGE TO "SHAMO THE MANSLAUGHTER WHALE."

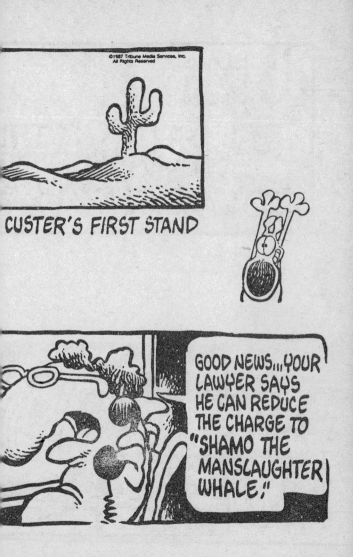

OH, PLEASE, MOM... IT'S GOT FRAGMENTS OF BOLL WEEVIL LARVAE AND RODENT HAIRS IN EVERY BOX.
CAPT'N SLIME
12-20

BEDS

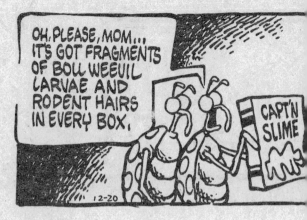

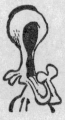

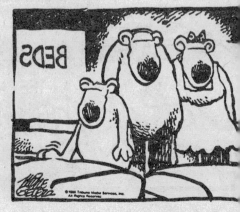

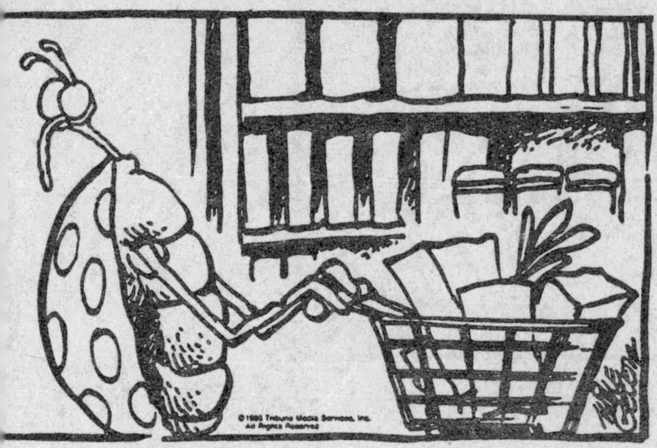

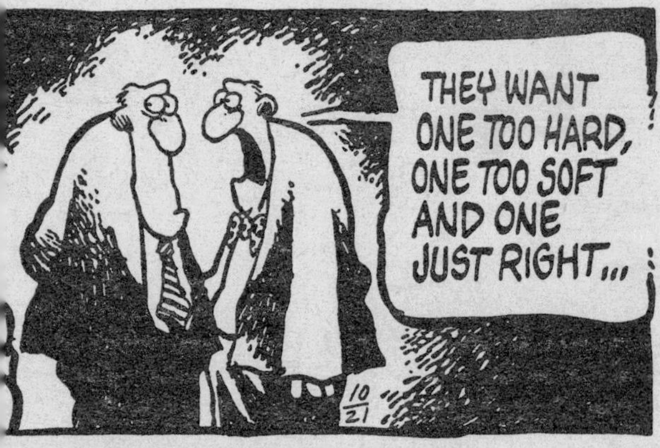
THEY WANT ONE TOO HARD, ONE TOO SOFT AND ONE JUST RIGHT...
10/21

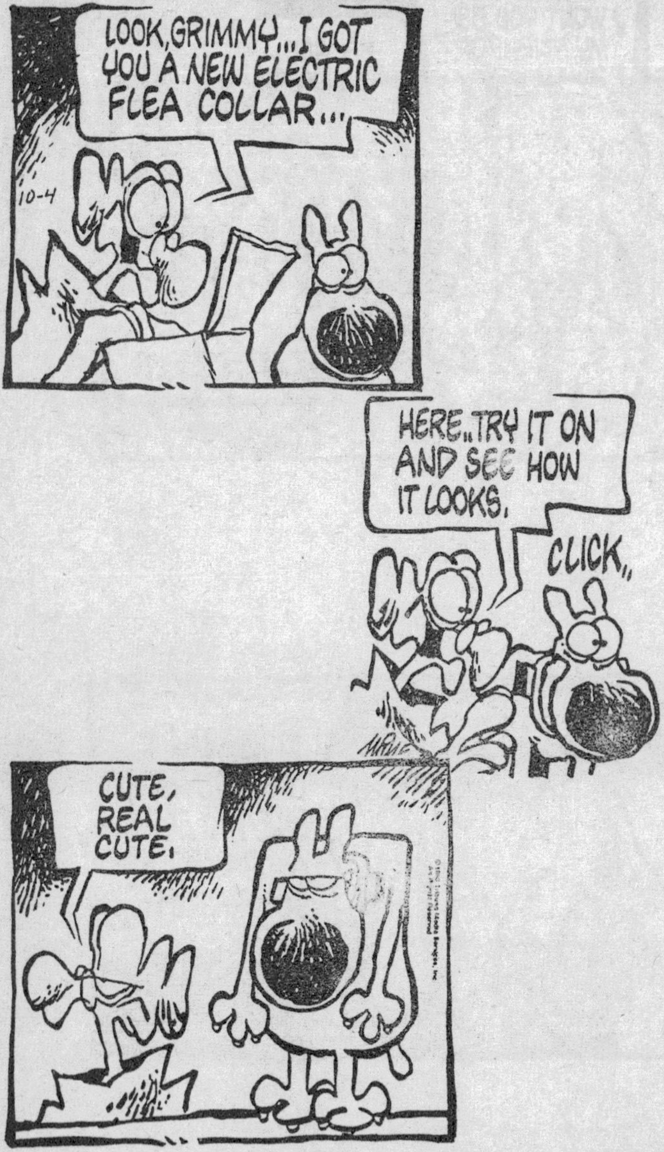
10-4
LOOK, GRIMMY...I GOT YOU A NEW ELECTRIC FLEA COLLAR...
HERE..TRY IT ON AND SEE HOW IT LOOKS.
CLICK..
CUTE, REAL CUTE.

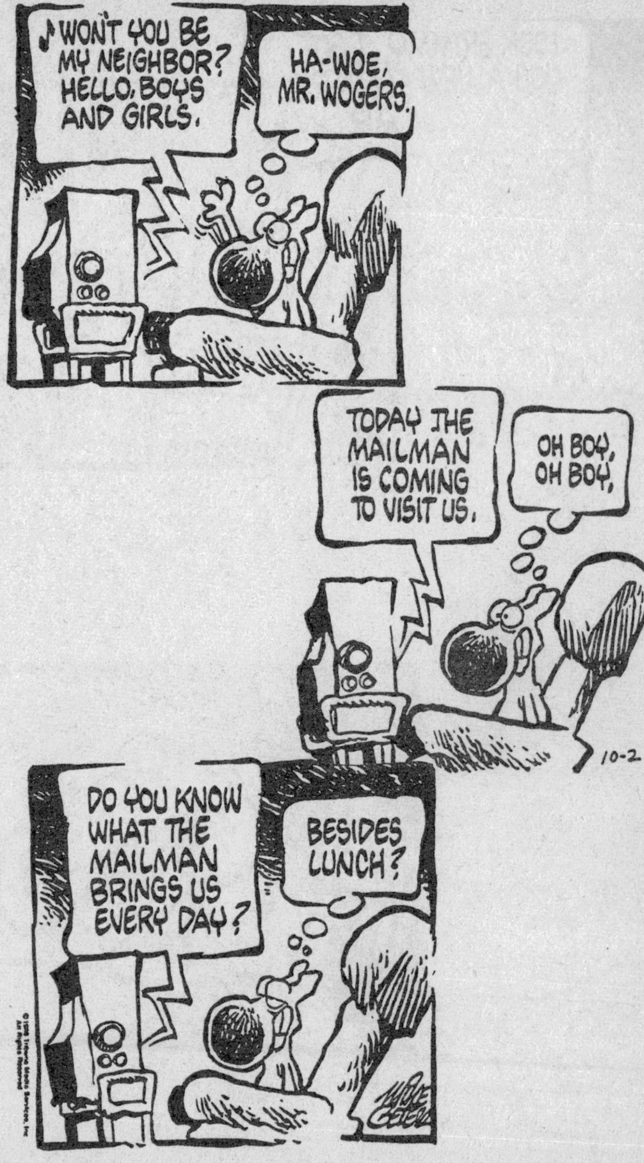
♪ WON'T YOU BE MY NEIGHBOR? HELLO, BOYS AND GIRLS.
HA-WOE, MR. WOGERS.
TODAY THE MAILMAN IS COMING TO VISIT US.
OH BOY, OH BOY.
10-2
DO YOU KNOW WHAT THE MAILMAN BRINGS US EVERY DAY?
BESIDES LUNCH?
Tribune Media Services, Inc. All Rights Reserved

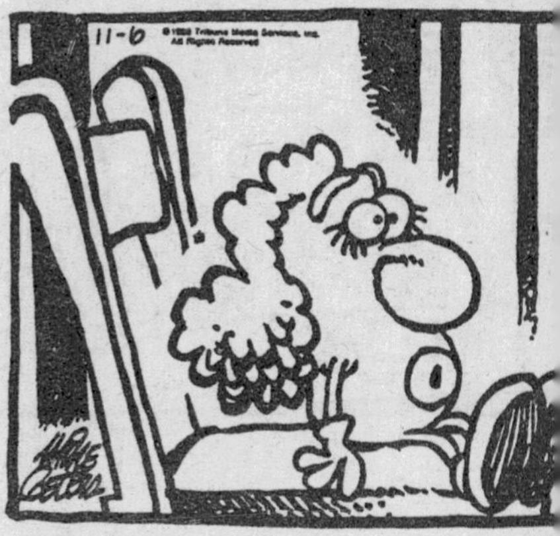
11-6
Tribune Media Services, Inc.
All Rights Reserved

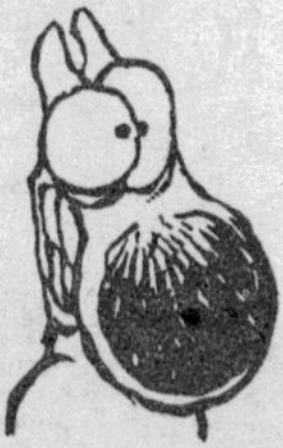

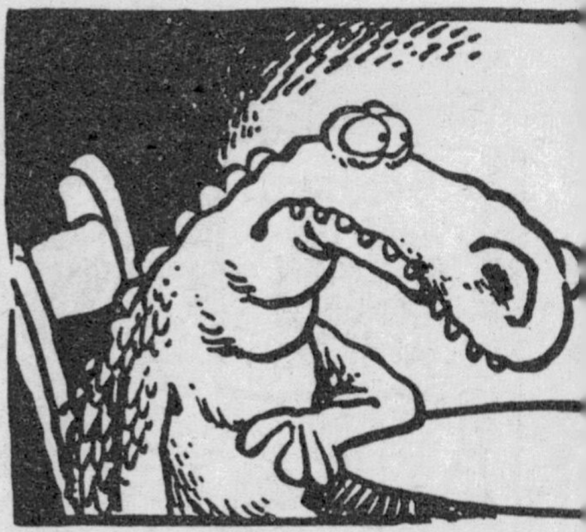

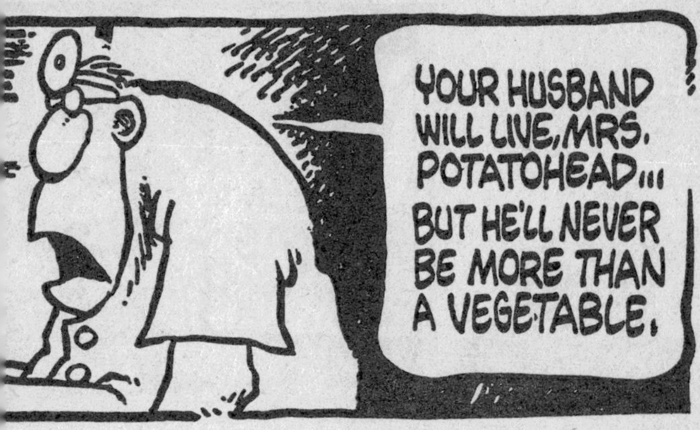
YOUR HUSBAND WILL LIVE, MRS. POTATOHEAD... BUT HE'LL NEVER BE MORE THAN A VEGETABLE.

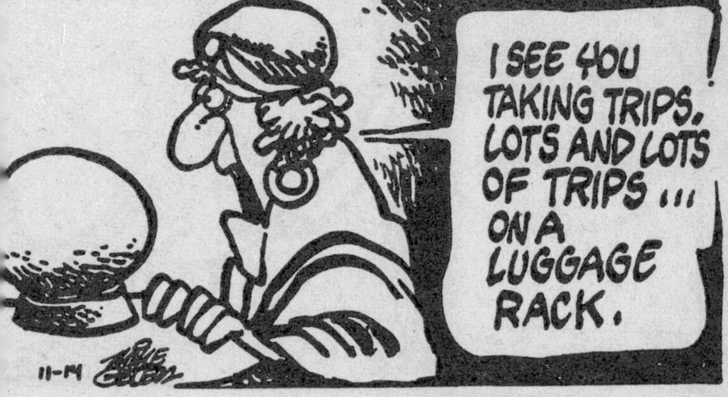
I SEE YOU TAKING TRIPS. LOTS AND LOTS OF TRIPS... ON A LUGGAGE RACK.
11-14

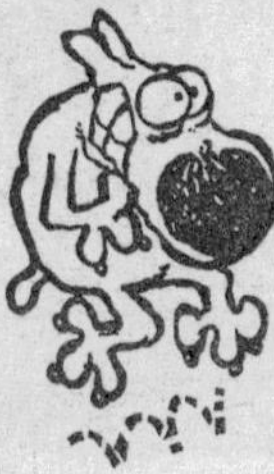

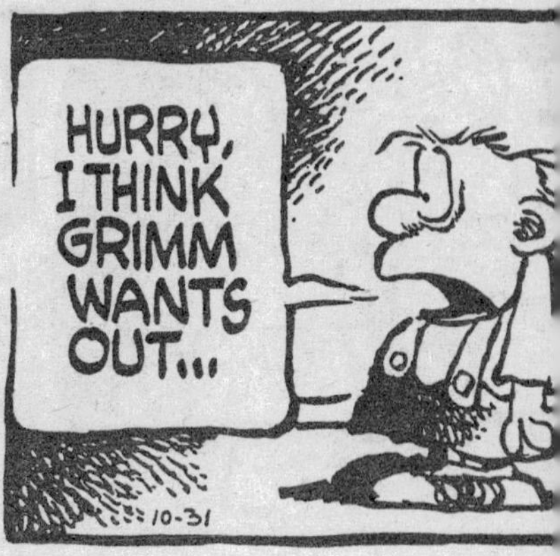
HURRY, I THINK GRIMM WANTS OUT...
10-31

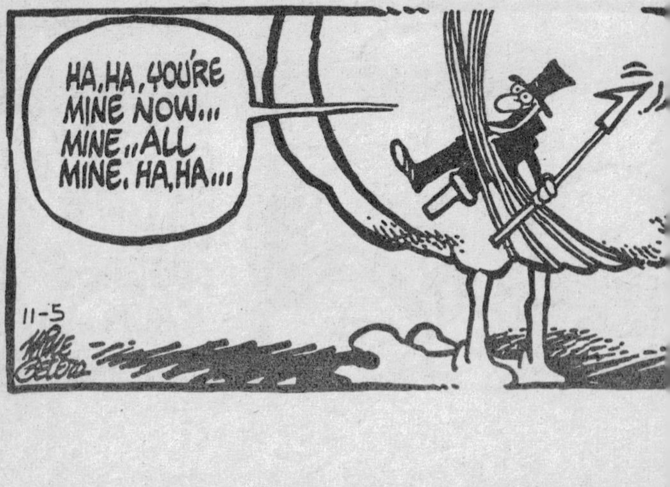
HA,HA, YOU'RE MINE NOW... MINE.. ALL MINE. HA,HA...
11-5

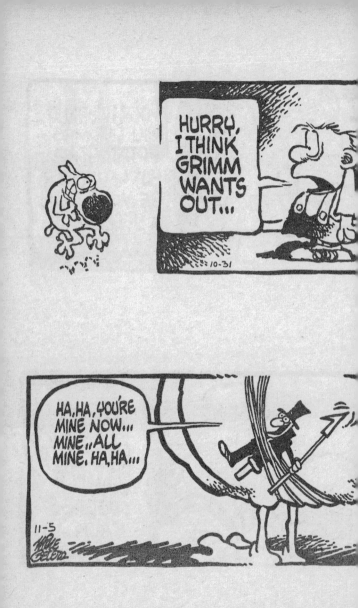

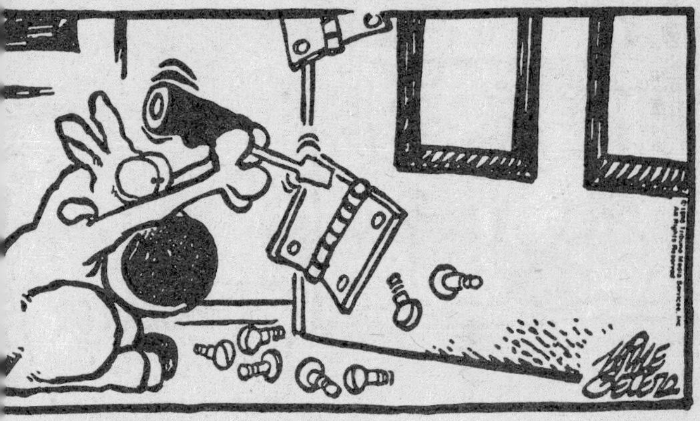

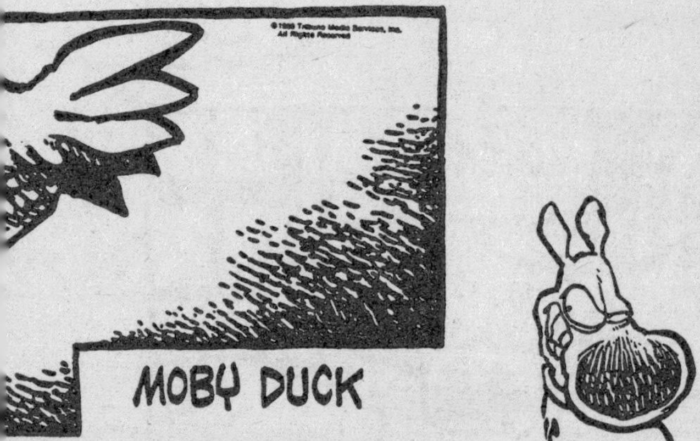
MOBY DUCK

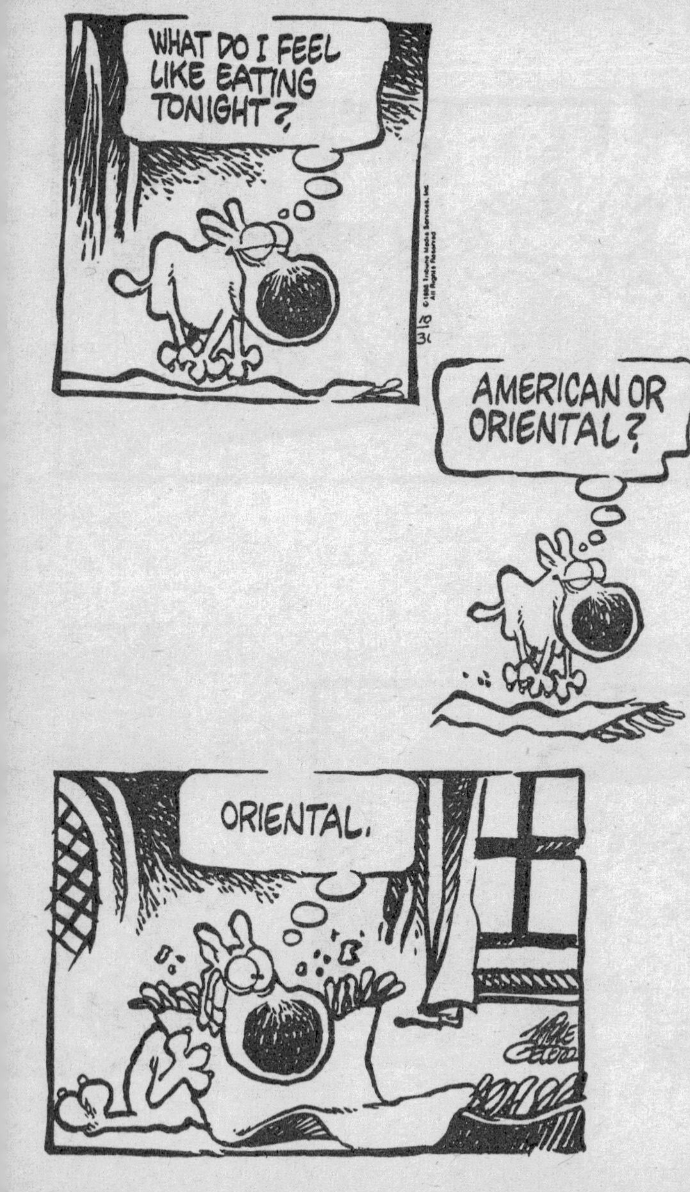
WHAT DO I FEEL LIKE EATING TONIGHT?
©1988 Tribune Media Services, Inc. All Rights Reserved
10/31
AMERICAN OR ORIENTAL?
ORIENTAL.

SORRY, YOUR DOG IS INFESTED WITH 350 KINDS OF BUGS, TICKS AND FLEAS...
WELL, DO SOMETHING!
6-19
I CAN'T...
HE'S NOW PROTECTED AS A NATIONAL WILDLIFE PRESERVE.

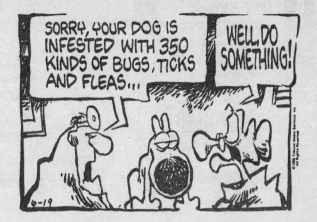

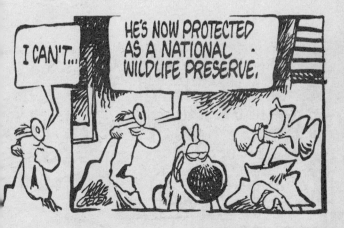

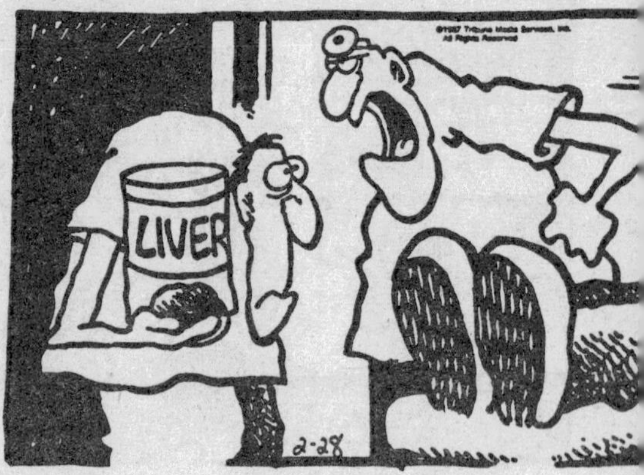
LIVER
2-28

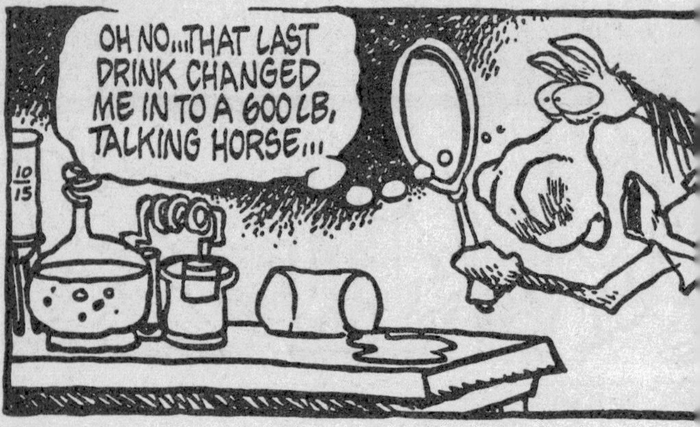
OH NO...THAT LAST DRINK CHANGED ME IN TO A 600 LB. TALKING HORSE...
10/15

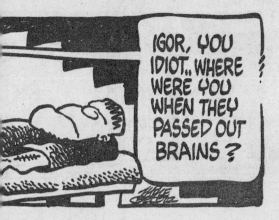

IGOR, YOU IDIOT.. WHERE WERE YOU WHEN THEY PASSED OUT BRAINS?

LAB

DR. JEKYLL AND MR. ED

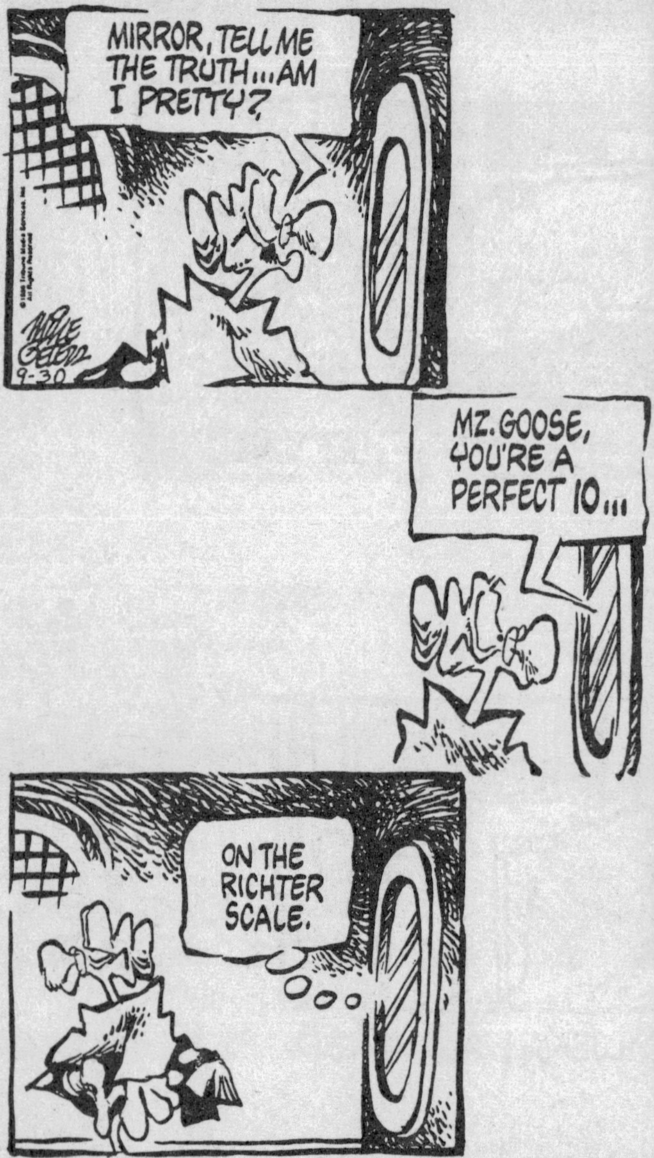
MIRROR, TELL ME THE TRUTH... AM I PRETTY?
MZ. GOOSE, YOU'RE A PERFECT 10...
ON THE RICHTER SCALE.

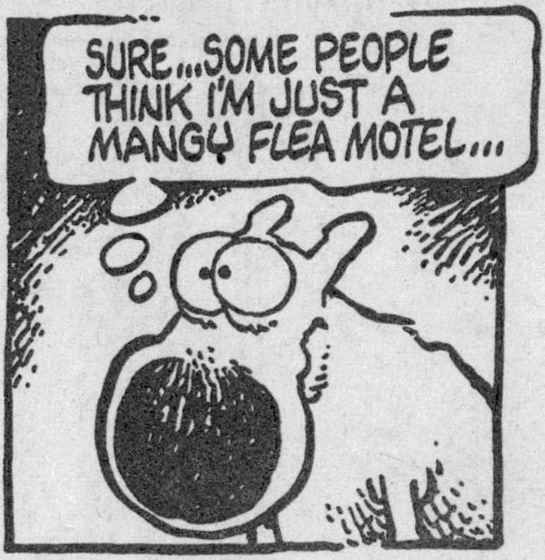
SURE...SOME PEOPLE THINK I'M JUST A MANGY FLEA MOTEL...

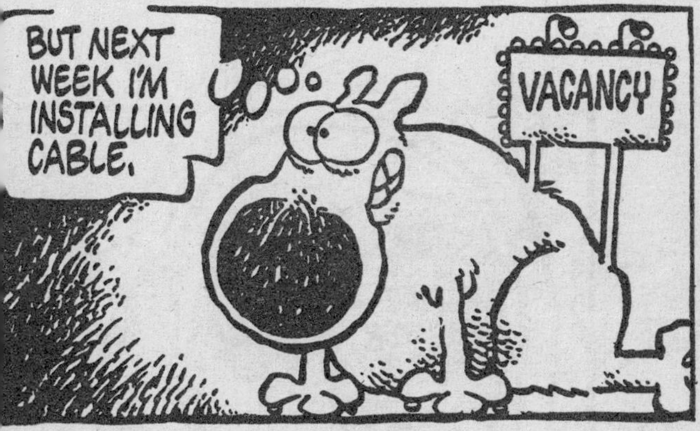
BUT NEXT WEEK I'M INSTALLING CABLE.
VACANCY

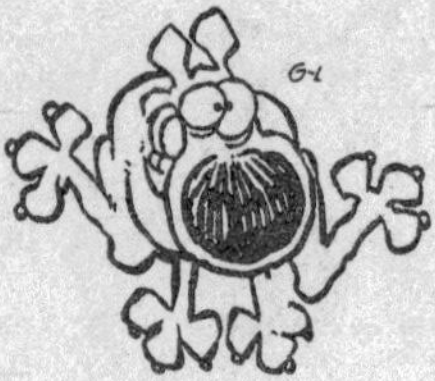

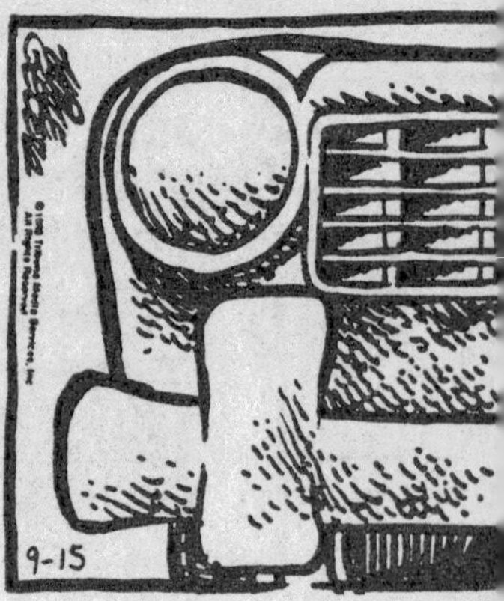
Tribune Media Services, Inc
All Rights Reserved
9-15

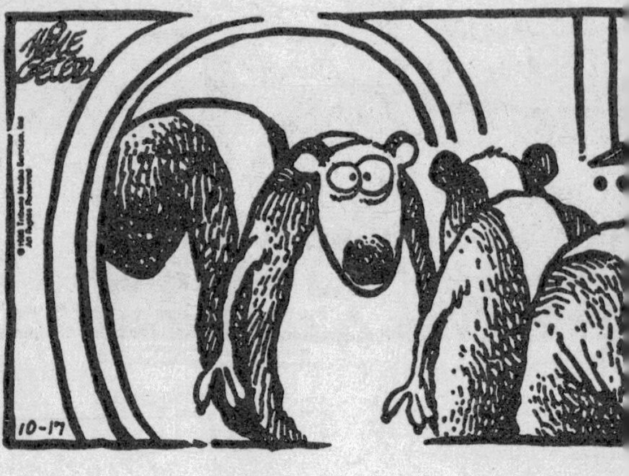
10-17

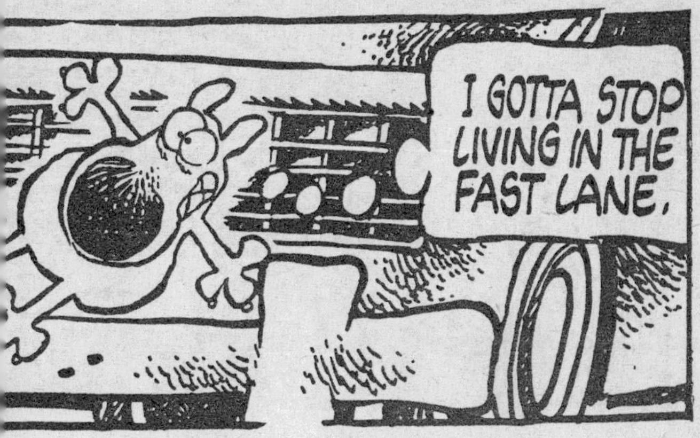
I GOTTA STOP LIVING IN THE FAST LANE.

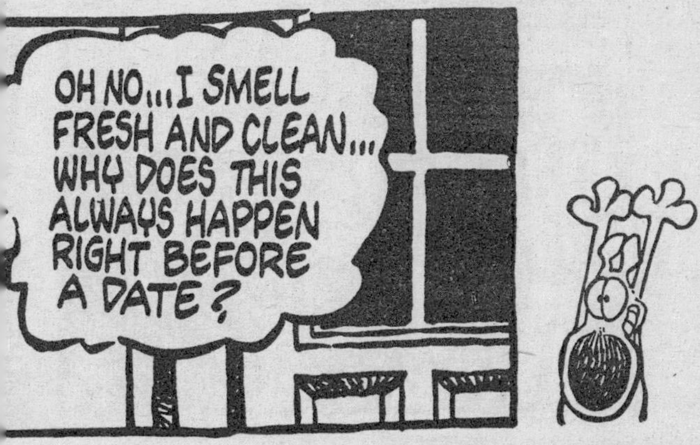
OH NO...I SMELL FRESH AND CLEAN... WHY DOES THIS ALWAYS HAPPEN RIGHT BEFORE A DATE?

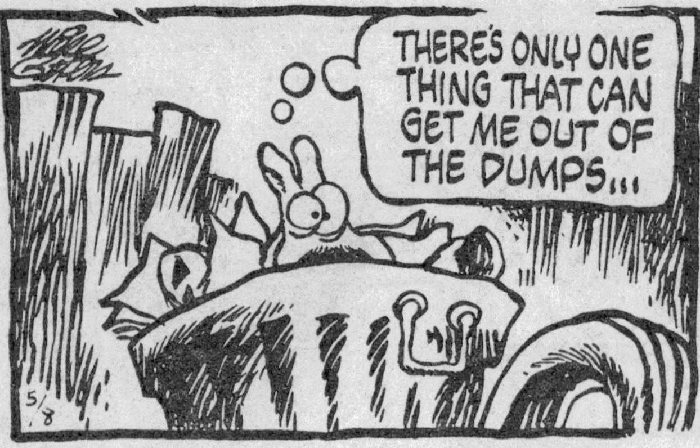
THERE'S ONLY ONE THING THAT CAN GET ME OUT OF THE DUMPS...
5/8

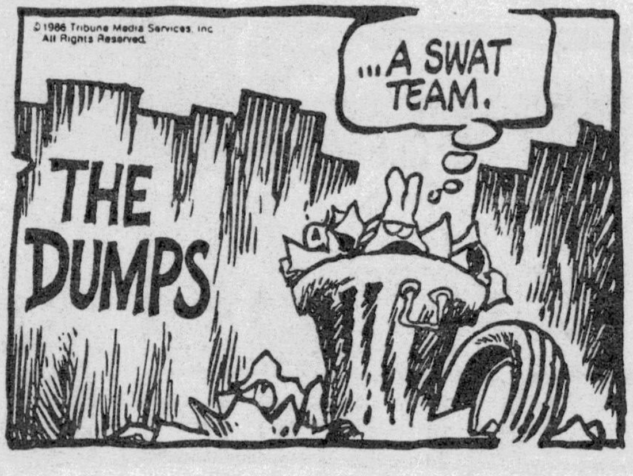
© 1986 Tribune Media Services, Inc
All Rights Reserved.
...A SWAT TEAM.
THE DUMPS

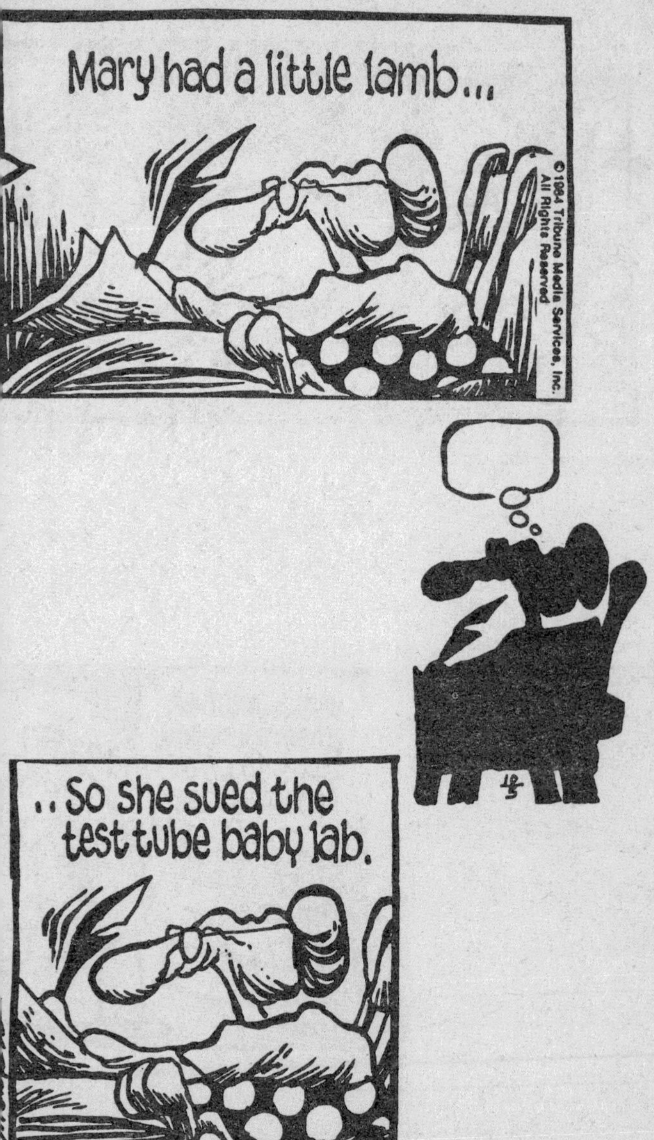
Mary had a little lamb...
© 1984 Tribune Media Services, Inc. All Rights Reserved
..So she sued the test tube baby lab.

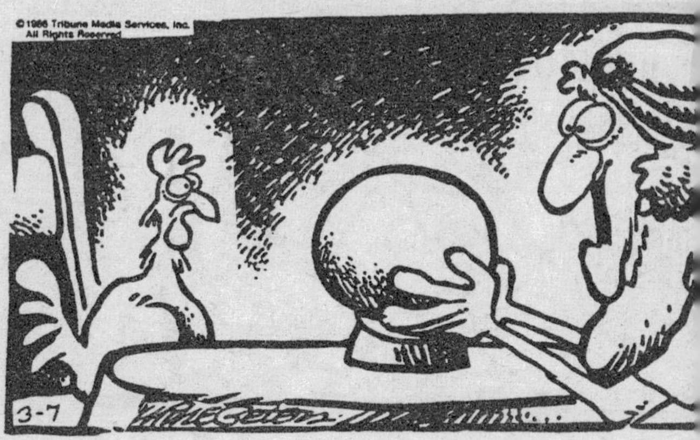
©1986 Tribune Media Services, Inc.
All Rights Reserved
3-7

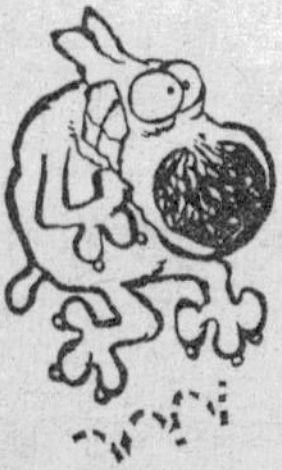

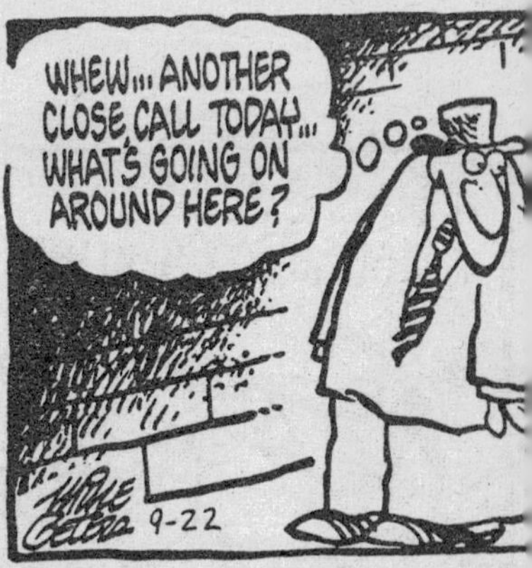
WHEW... ANOTHER CLOSE CALL TODAY... WHAT'S GOING ON AROUND HERE?
9-22

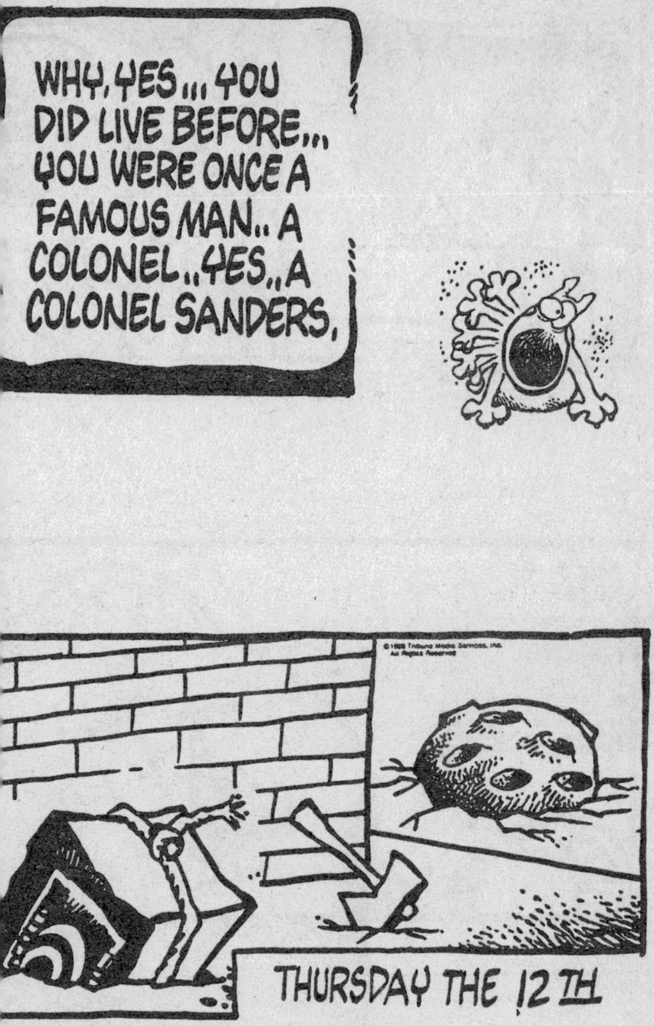
WHY, YES... YOU DID LIVE BEFORE... YOU WERE ONCE A FAMOUS MAN.. A COLONEL..YES.,A COLONEL SANDERS,
THURSDAY THE 12TH

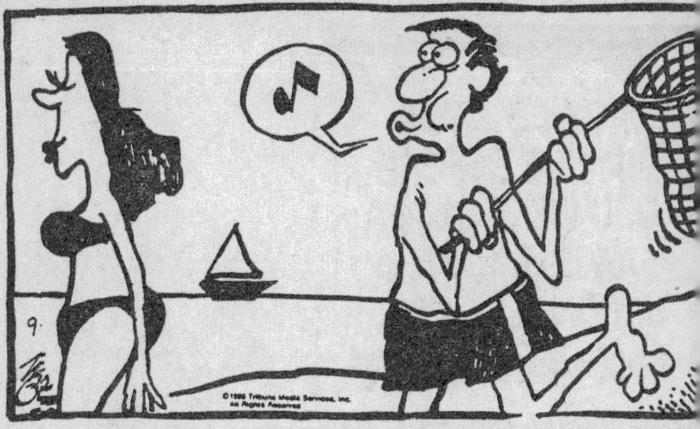
9.
©1986 Tribune Media Services, Inc.
All Rights Reserved

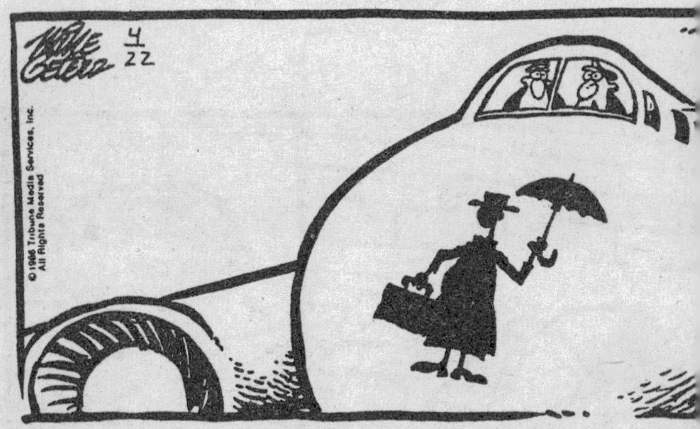
4/22
©1986 Tribune Media Services, Inc.
All Rights Reserved

BEACH PARTY

FRANKIE AND A NET

YEAH... I FELT A BUMP TOO.

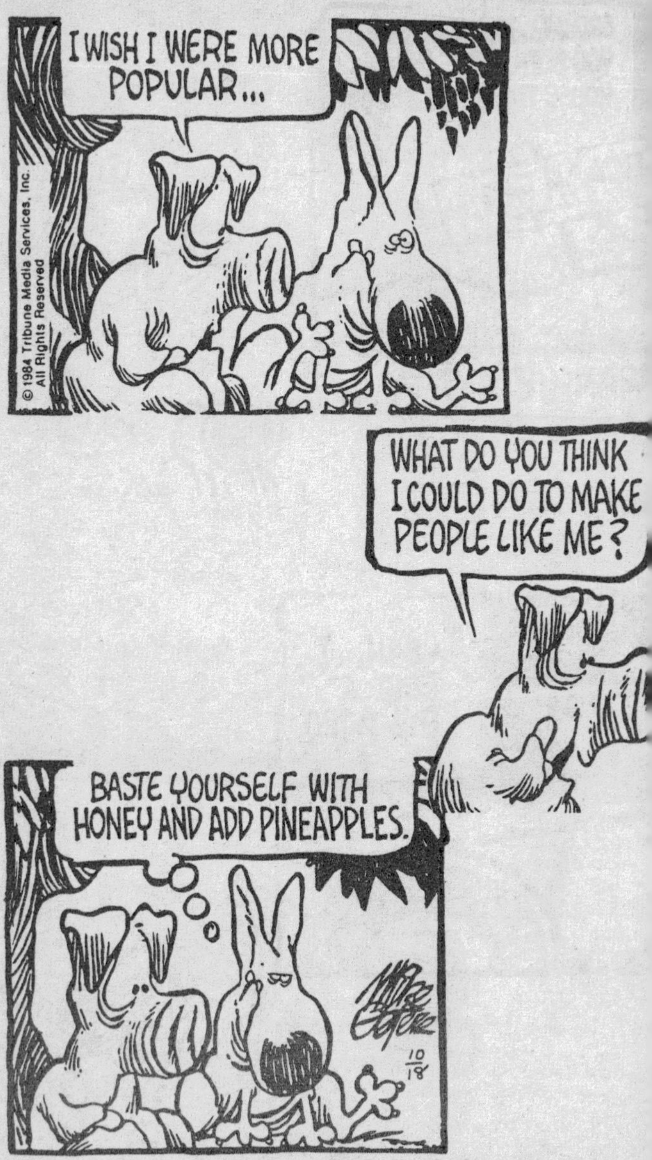

I WISH I WERE MORE POPULAR...
© 1984 Tribune Media Services, Inc.
All Rights Reserved
WHAT DO YOU THINK I COULD DO TO MAKE PEOPLE LIKE ME?
BASTE YOURSELF WITH HONEY AND ADD PINEAPPLES.
10/18

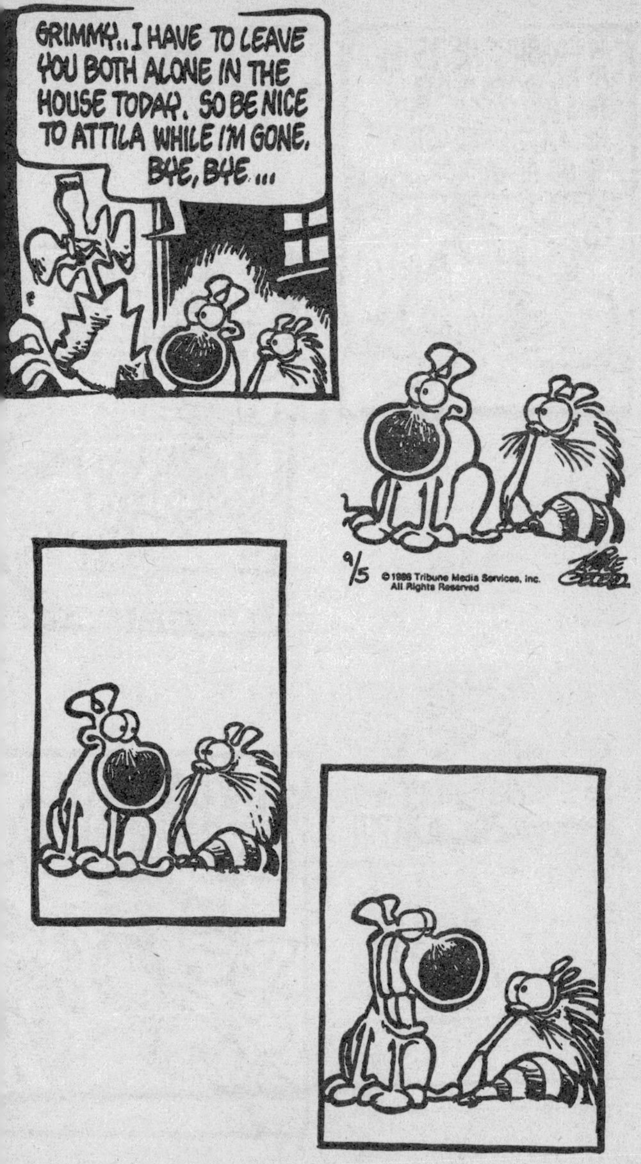
GRIMMY.. I HAVE TO LEAVE YOU BOTH ALONE IN THE HOUSE TODAY. SO BE NICE TO ATTILA WHILE I'M GONE.
BYE, BYE...
9/5
©1986 Tribune Media Services, Inc.
All Rights Reserved

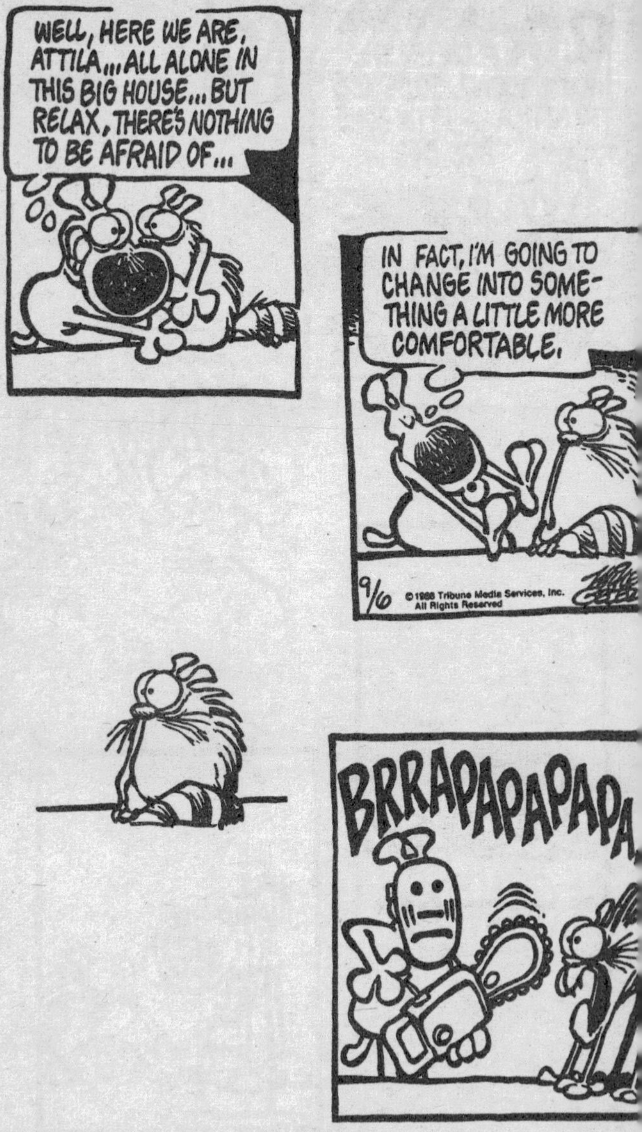
WELL, HERE WE ARE, ATTILA... ALL ALONE IN THIS BIG HOUSE... BUT RELAX, THERE'S NOTHING TO BE AFRAID OF...
IN FACT, I'M GOING TO CHANGE INTO SOMETHING A LITTLE MORE COMFORTABLE.
9/6
©1988 Tribune Media Services, Inc. All Rights Reserved
BRRAPAPAPAPA

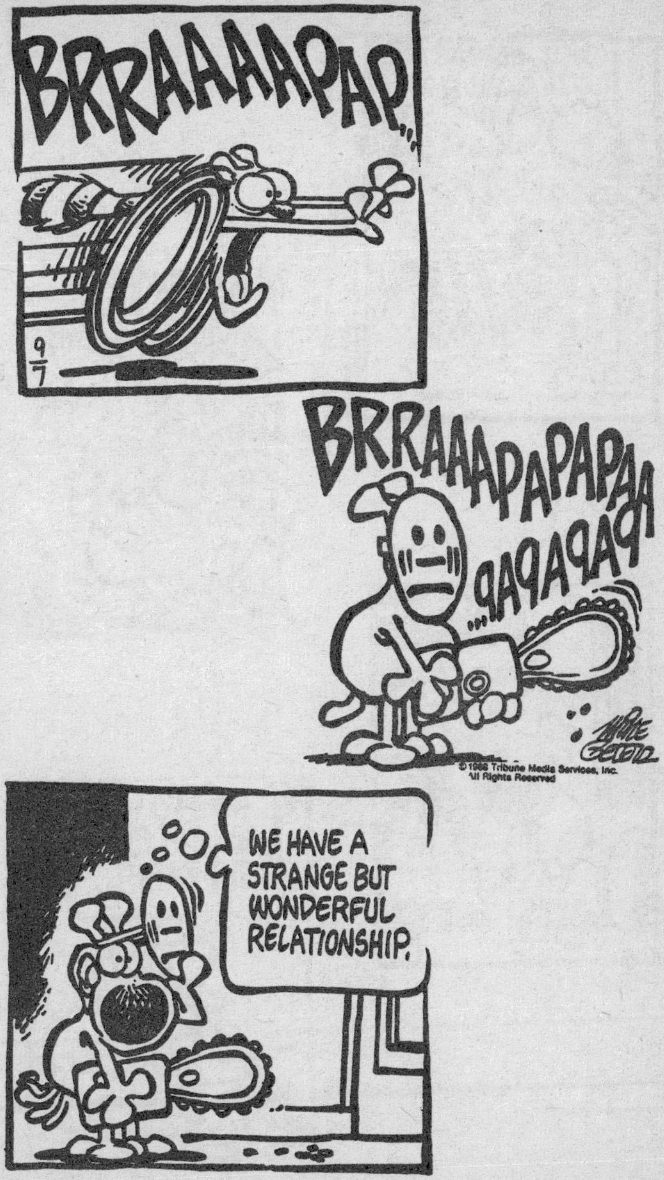
BRRAAAAPAP...
9/7
BRRAAAPAPAPAA
PAPAPAP...
WE HAVE A STRANGE BUT WONDERFUL RELATIONSHIP.

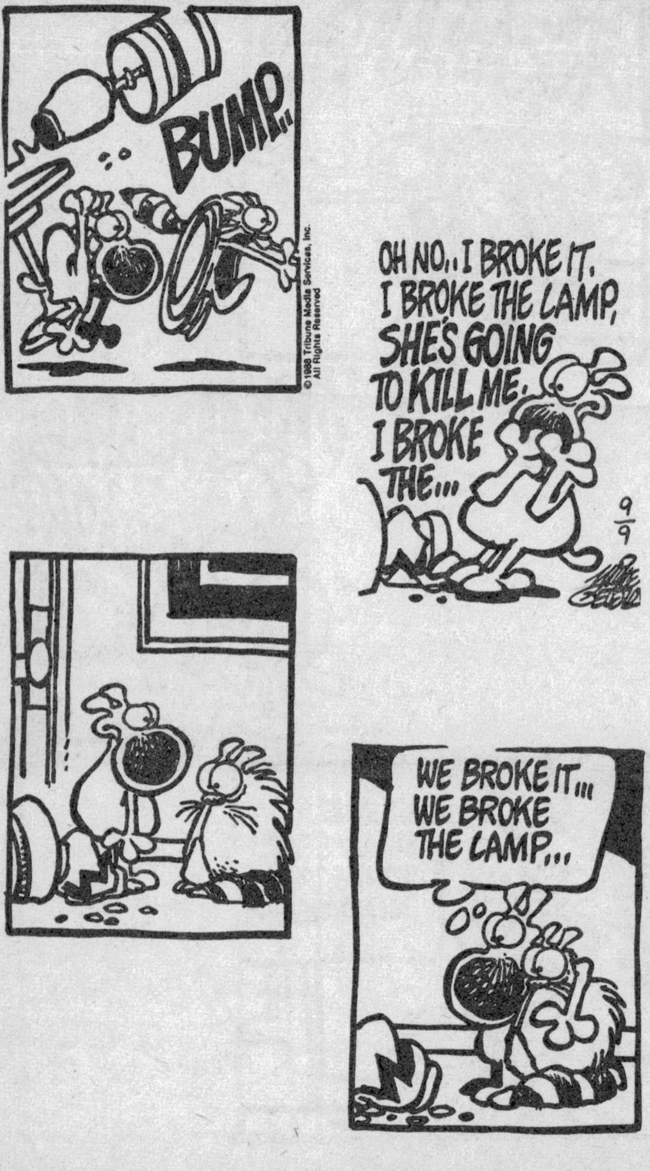
BUMP..
©1988 Tribune Media Services, Inc.
All Rights Reserved
WE BROKE IT... WE BROKE THE LAMP...
OH NO.. I BROKE IT. I BROKE THE LAMP, SHE'S GOING TO KILL ME. I BROKE THE...
9/9

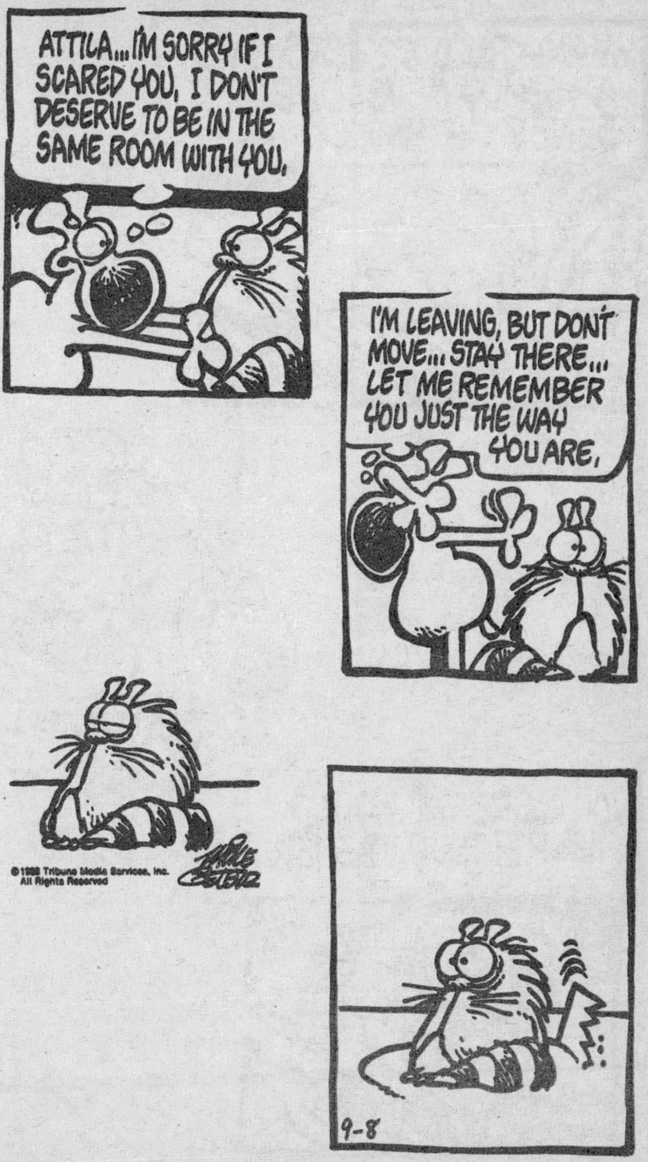
ATTILA... I'M SORRY IF I SCARED YOU. I DON'T DESERVE TO BE IN THE SAME ROOM WITH YOU.
I'M LEAVING, BUT DON'T MOVE... STAY THERE... LET ME REMEMBER YOU JUST THE WAY YOU ARE.
Tribune Media Services, Inc.
All Rights Reserved
9-8

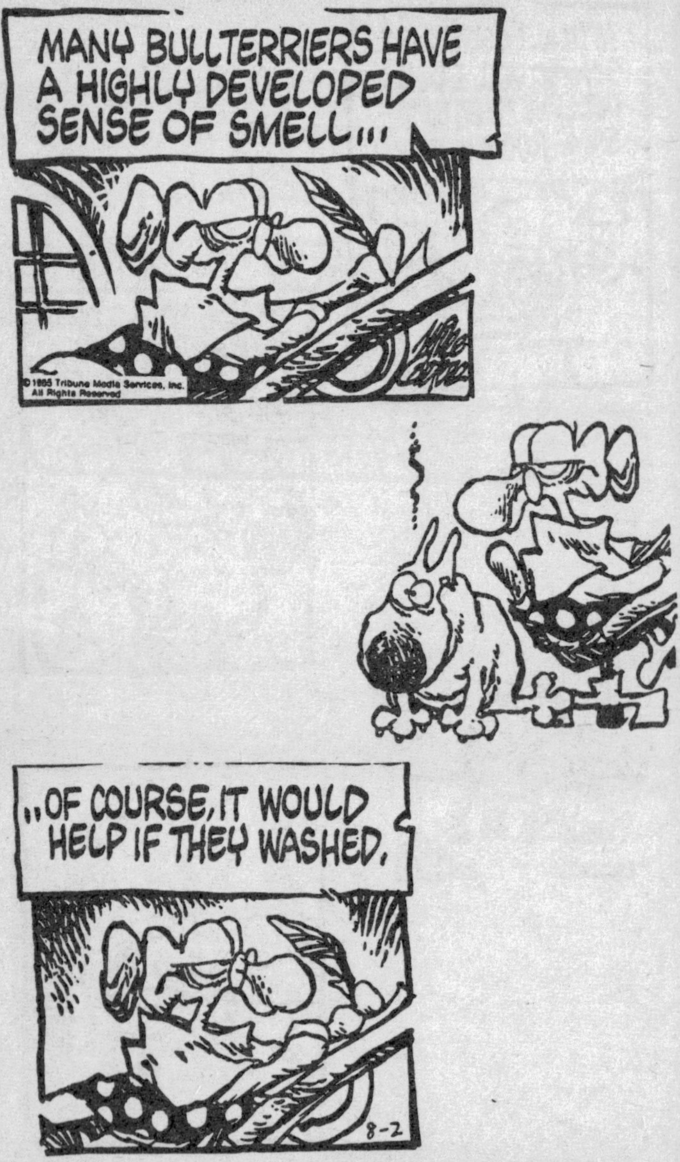
MANY BULLTERRIERS HAVE A HIGHLY DEVELOPED SENSE OF SMELL...
© 1985 Tribune Media Services, Inc. All Rights Reserved
...OF COURSE, IT WOULD HELP IF THEY WASHED.
8-2

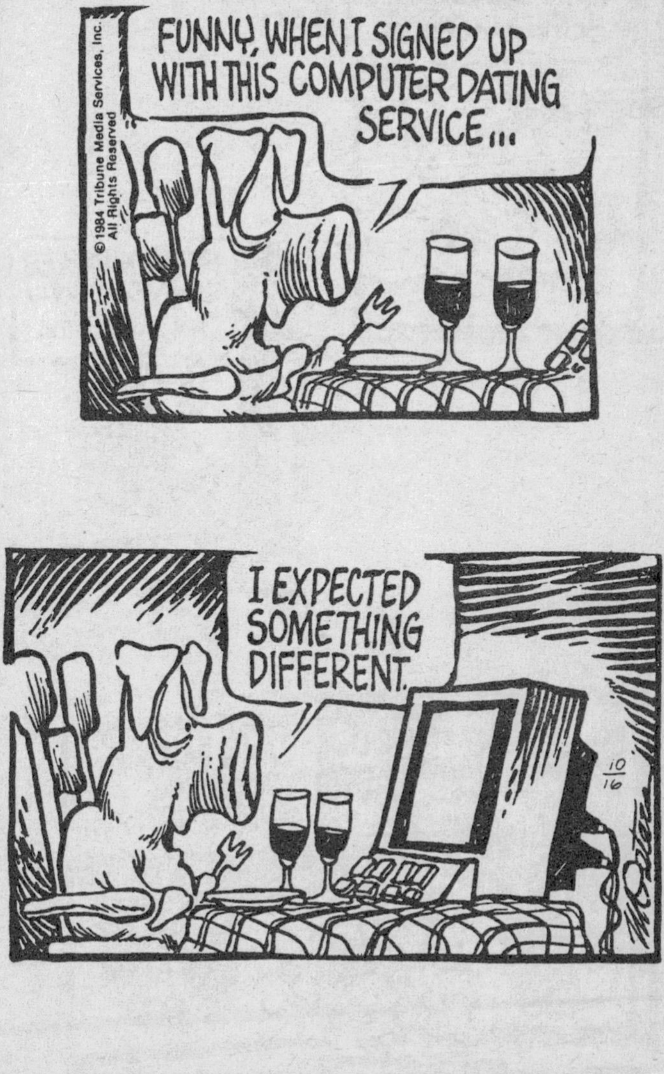
FUNNY, WHEN I SIGNED UP WITH THIS COMPUTER DATING SERVICE...
I EXPECTED SOMETHING DIFFERENT.
©1984 Tribune Media Services, Inc. All Rights Reserved
10/16

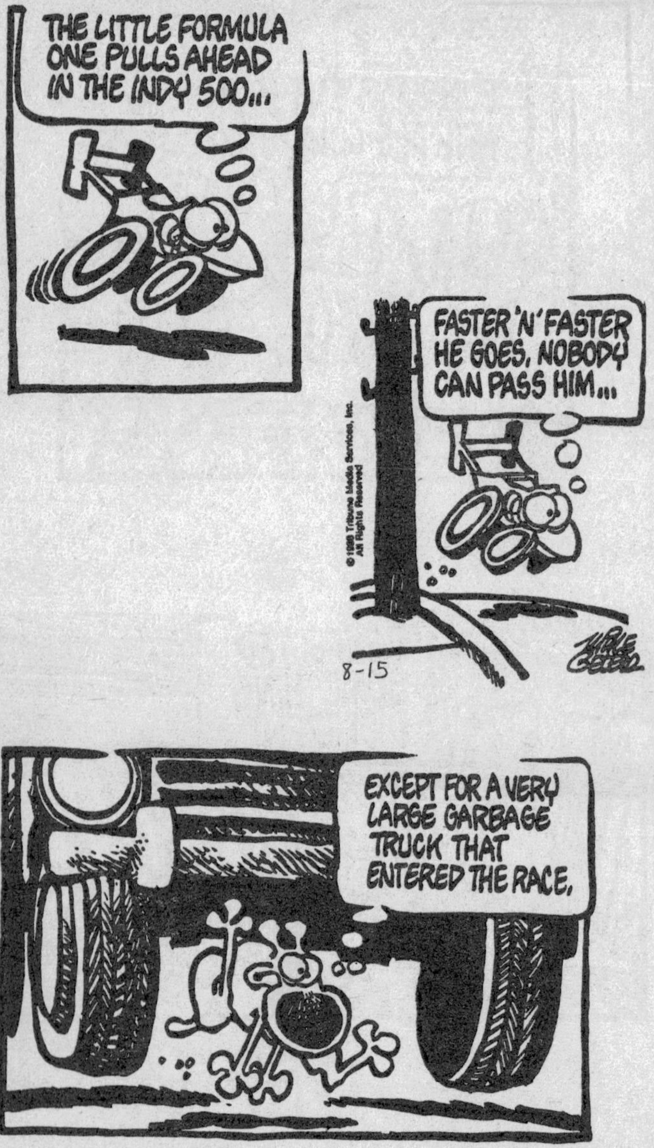
THE LITTLE FORMULA ONE PULLS AHEAD IN THE INDY 500...
FASTER 'N' FASTER HE GOES, NOBODY CAN PASS HIM...
© Tribune Media Services, Inc. All Rights Reserved
8-15
EXCEPT FOR A VERY LARGE GARBAGE TRUCK THAT ENTERED THE RACE.

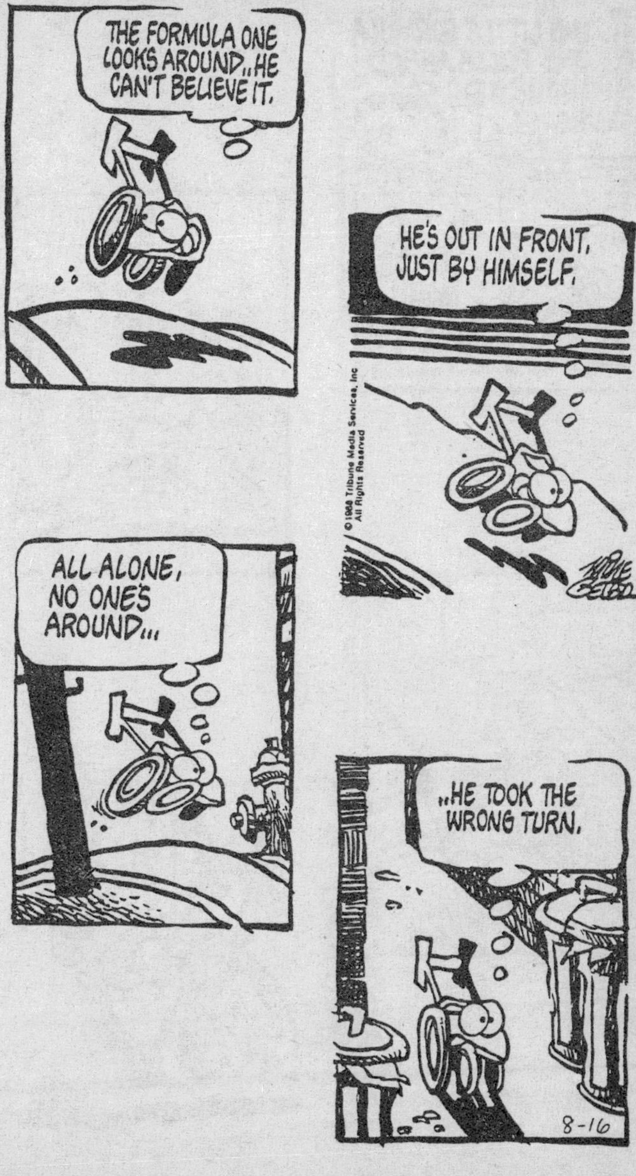
THE FORMULA ONE LOOKS AROUND.. HE CAN'T BELIEVE IT.
HE'S OUT IN FRONT, JUST BY HIMSELF.
© 1988 Tribune Media Services, Inc All Rights Reserved
ALL ALONE, NO ONE'S AROUND...
..HE TOOK THE WRONG TURN.
8-16

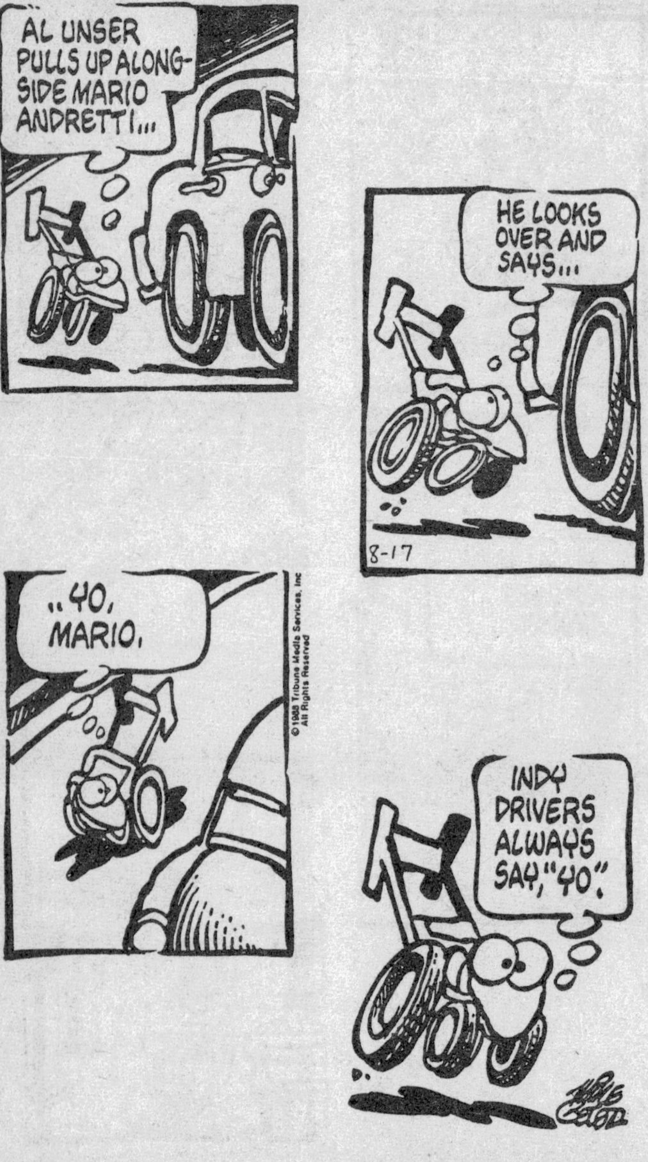
AL UNSER PULLS UP ALONGSIDE MARIO ANDRETTI...
HE LOOKS OVER AND SAYS...
8-17
..YO, MARIO.
INDY DRIVERS ALWAYS SAY, "YO".
© 1988 Tribune Media Services, Inc All Rights Reserved

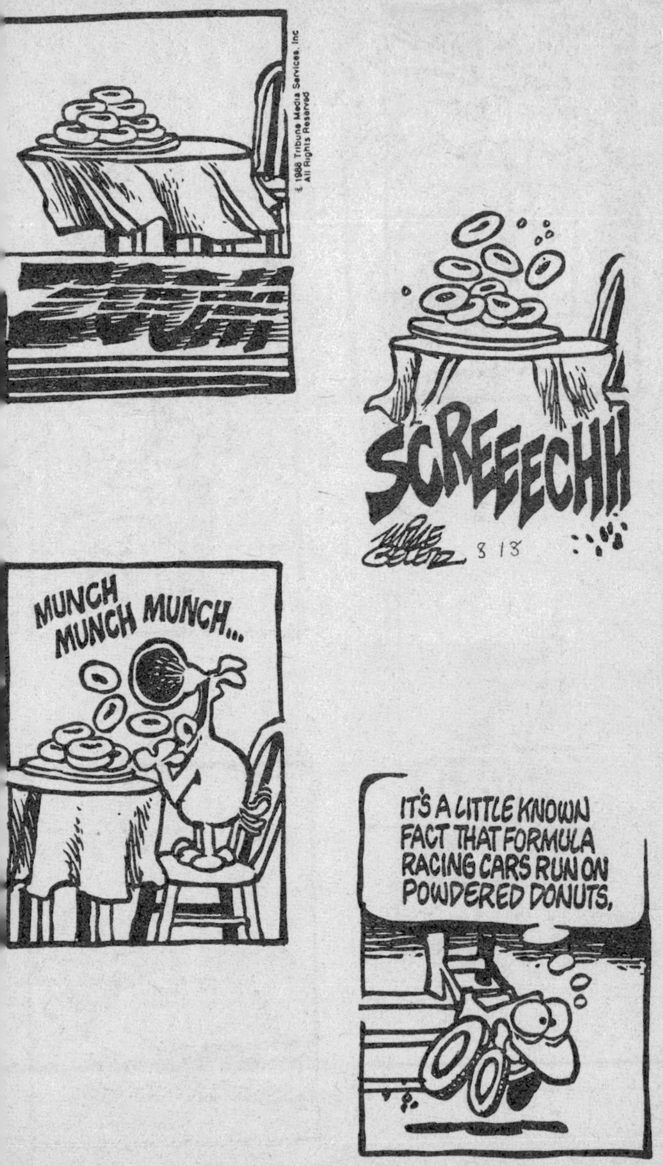
IT'S A LITTLE KNOWN FACT THAT FORMULA RACING CARS RUN ON POWDERED DONUTS.
MUNCH MUNCH MUNCH...
SCREEECHH
8 13
© 1988 Tribune Media Services, Inc
All Rights Reserved

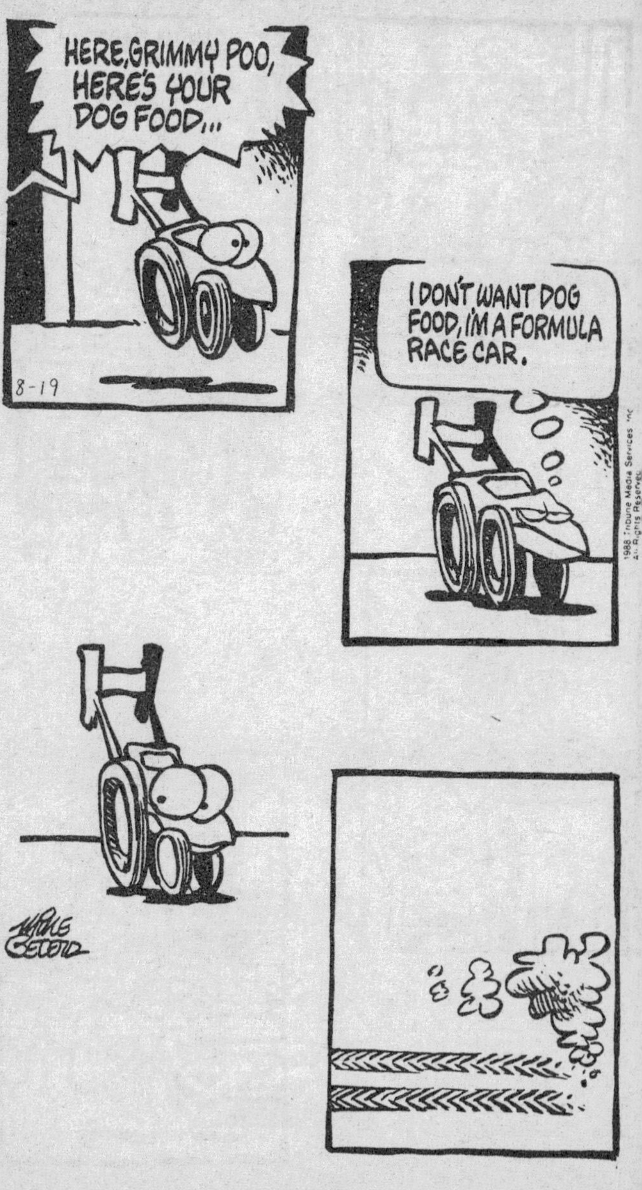
HERE, GRIMMY POO, HERE'S YOUR DOG FOOD...
8-19
I DON'T WANT DOG FOOD, I'M A FORMULA RACE CAR.
1988 Tribune Media Services Inc
All Rights Reserved

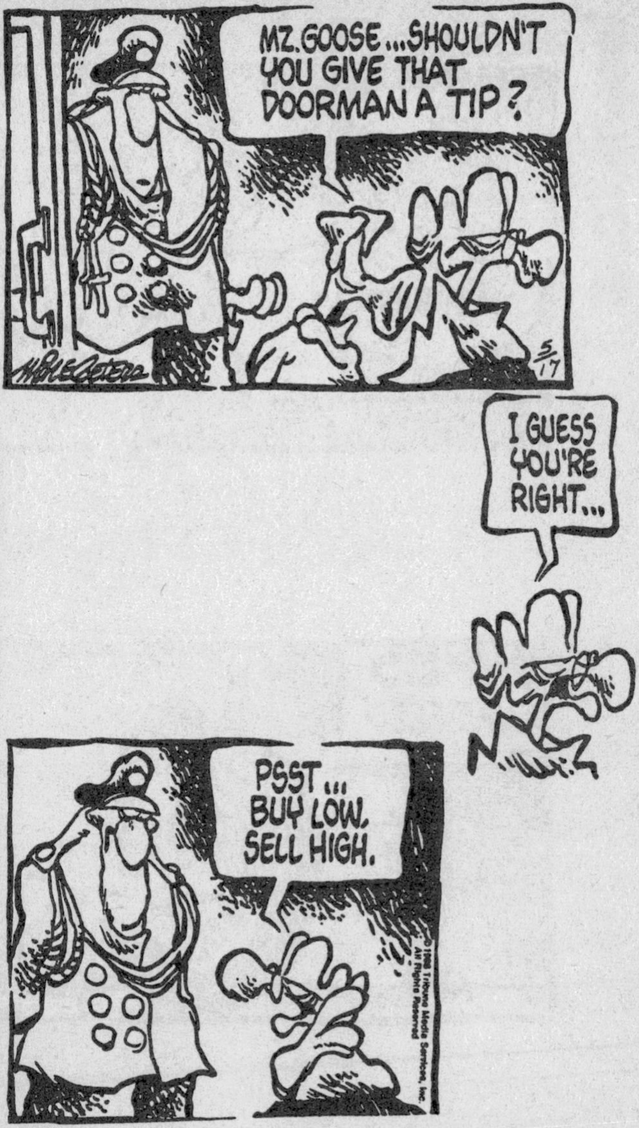
MZ. GOOSE ...SHOULDN'T YOU GIVE THAT DOORMAN A TIP?
5/17
I GUESS YOU'RE RIGHT...
PSST... BUY LOW. SELL HIGH.
©1988 Tribune Media Services, Inc. All Rights Reserved

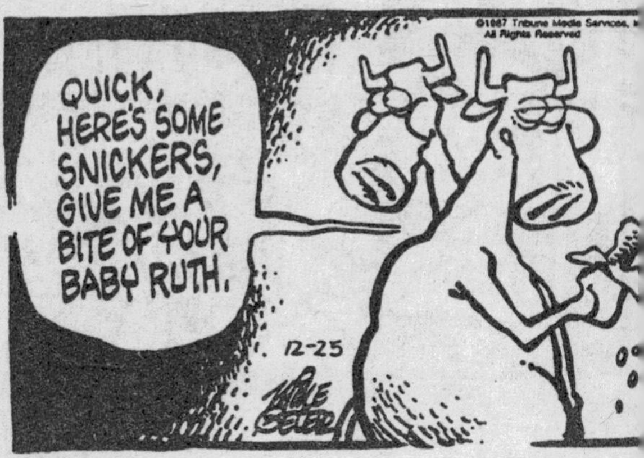
©1987 Tribune Media Services, Inc.
All Rights Reserved
QUICK, HERE'S SOME SNICKERS, GIVE ME A BITE OF YOUR BABY RUTH.
12-25

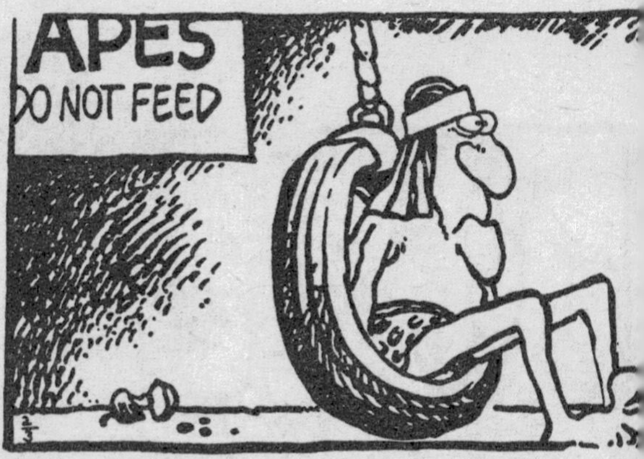
APES
DO NOT FEED

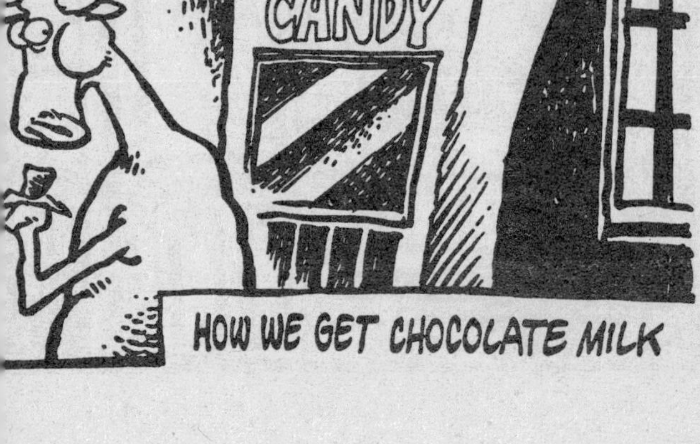
CANDY
HOW WE GET CHOCOLATE MILK

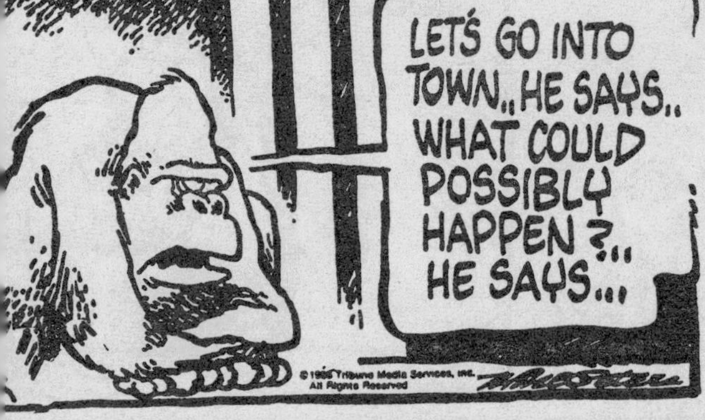
LET'S GO INTO TOWN.. HE SAYS.. WHAT COULD POSSIBLY HAPPEN ?.. HE SAYS...
Tribune Media Services, Inc.
All Rights Reserved

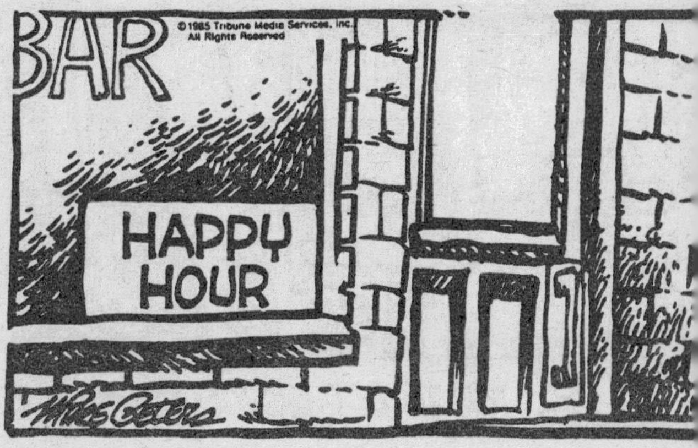
BAR
©1985 Tribune Media Services, Inc.
All Rights Reserved
HAPPY HOUR

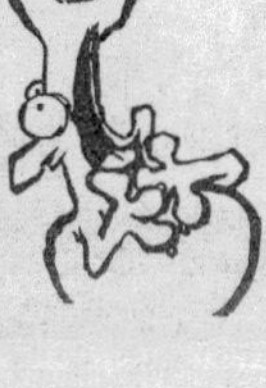

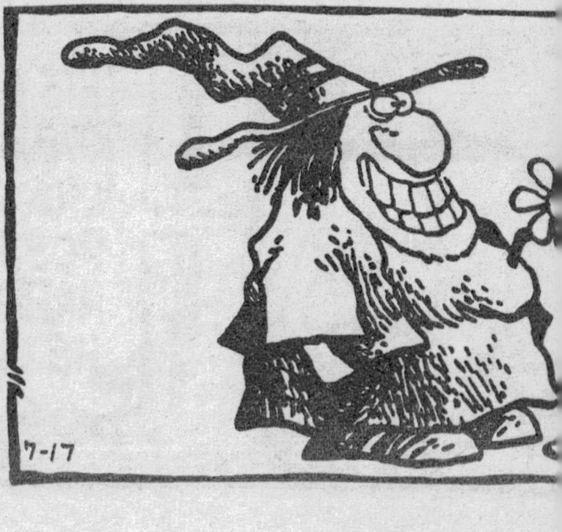
7-17

12-12

CRUEL WITCH JOKES

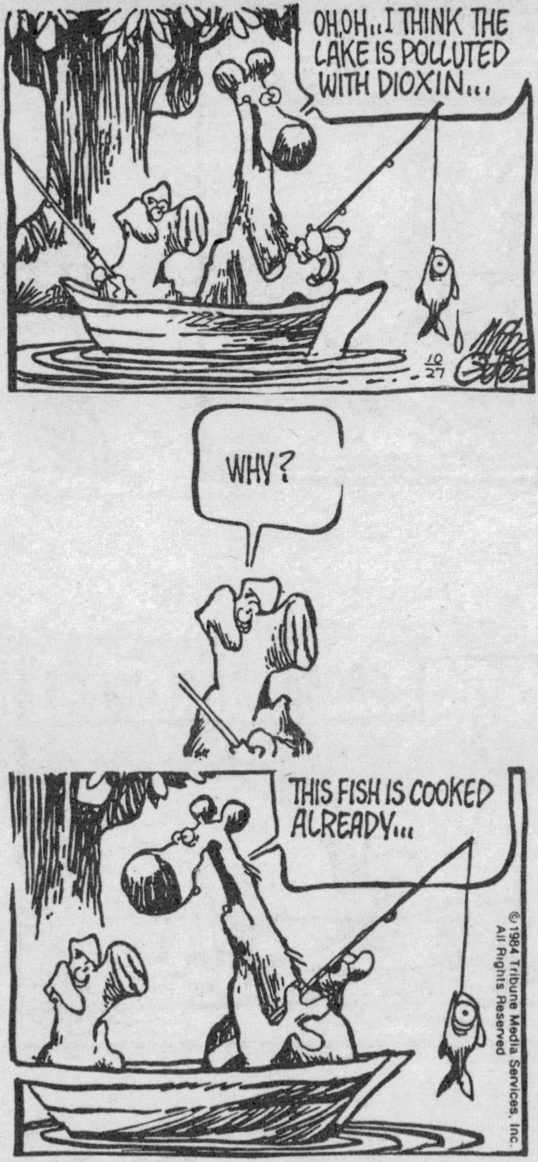
OH,OH..I THINK THE LAKE IS POLLUTED WITH DIOXIN...
WHY?
THIS FISH IS COOKED ALREADY...
© 1984 Tribune Media Services, Inc.
All Rights Reserved

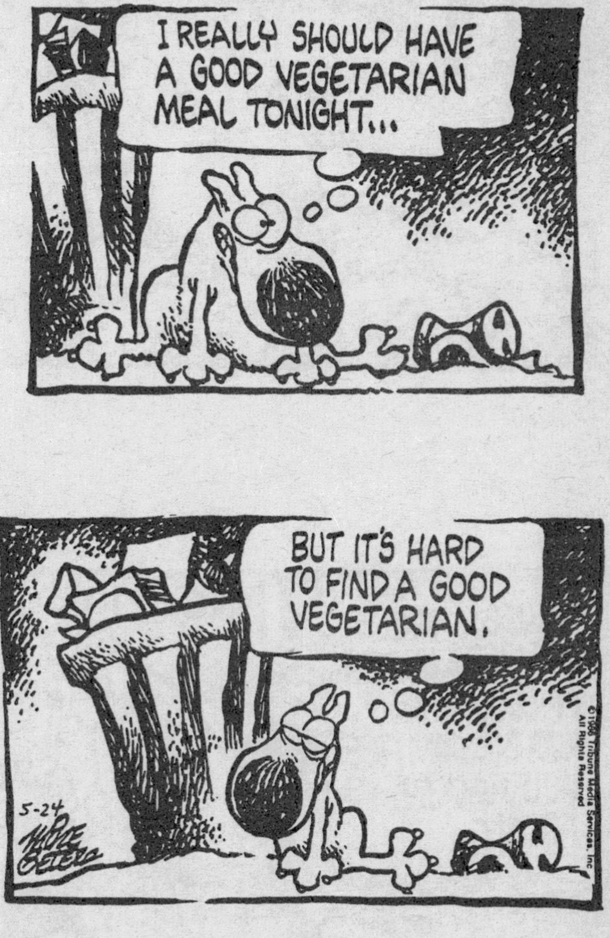
I REALLY SHOULD HAVE A GOOD VEGETARIAN MEAL TONIGHT...
BUT IT'S HARD TO FIND A GOOD VEGETARIAN.
5-24
Tribune Media Services, Inc
All Rights Reserved

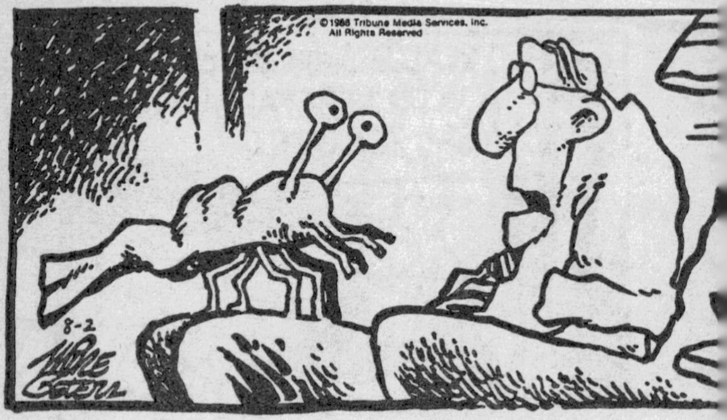
©1988 Tribune Media Services, Inc.
All Rights Reserved
8-2

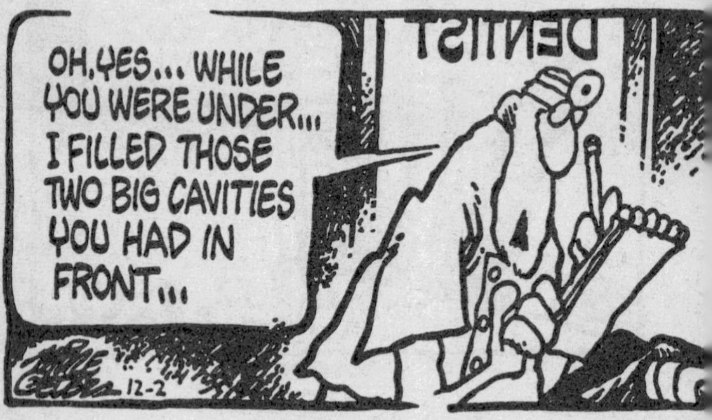
OH, YES... WHILE YOU WERE UNDER... I FILLED THOSE TWO BIG CAVITIES YOU HAD IN FRONT...
DENTIST
12-2

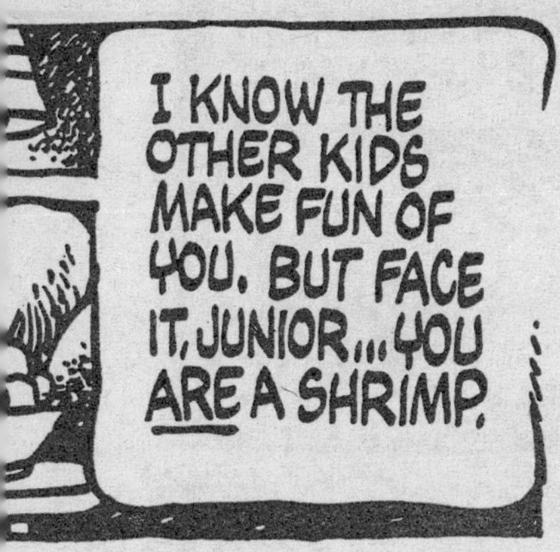
I KNOW THE OTHER KIDS MAKE FUN OF YOU. BUT FACE IT, JUNIOR... YOU ARE A SHRIMP.

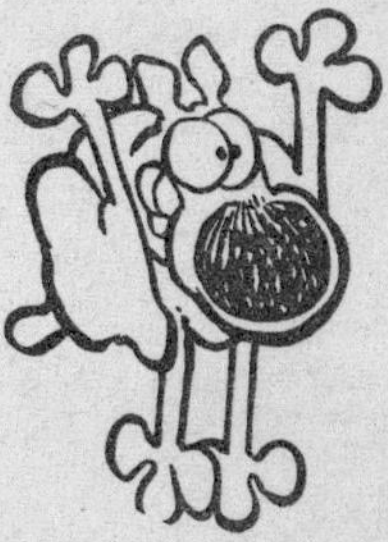

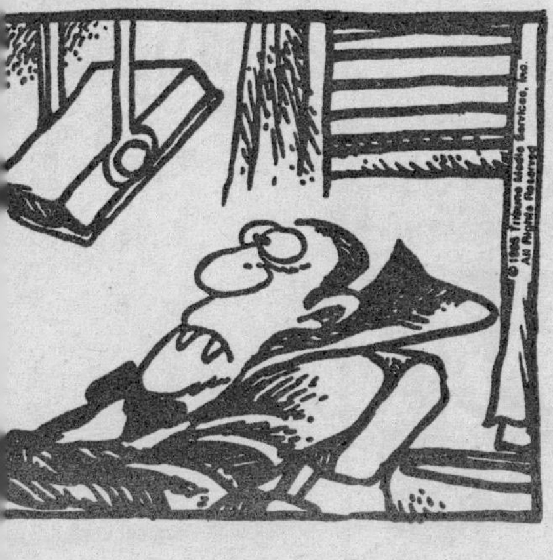
Tribune Media Services, Inc.
All Rights Reserved

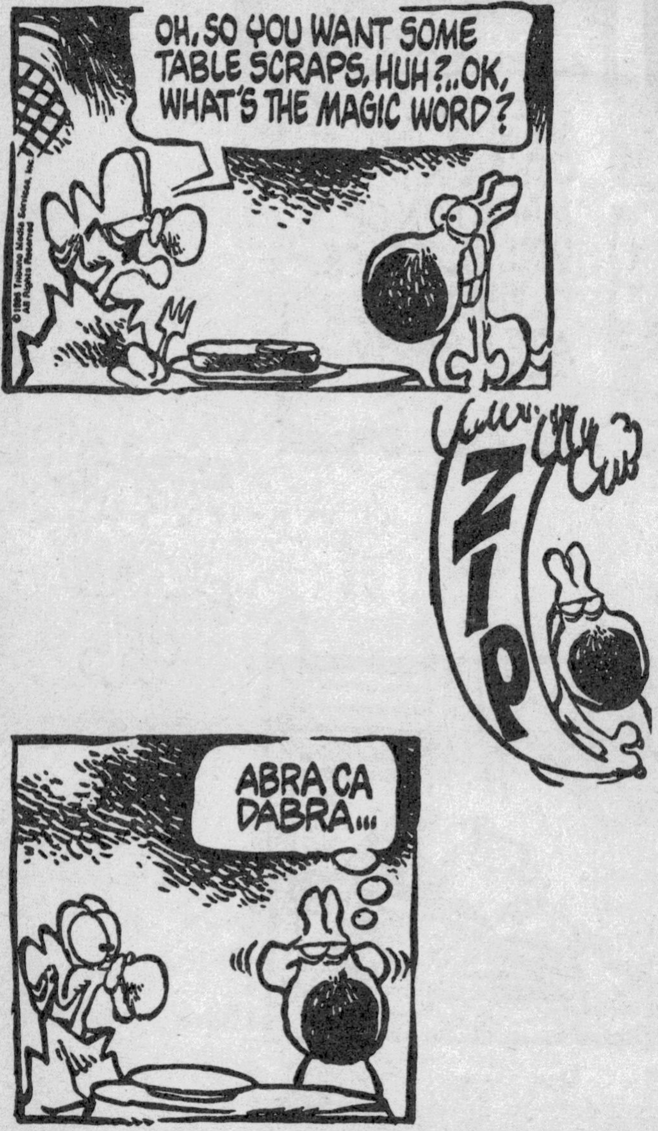
OH, SO YOU WANT SOME TABLE SCRAPS, HUH?..OK, WHAT'S THE MAGIC WORD?
ZIP
ABRA CA DABRA...

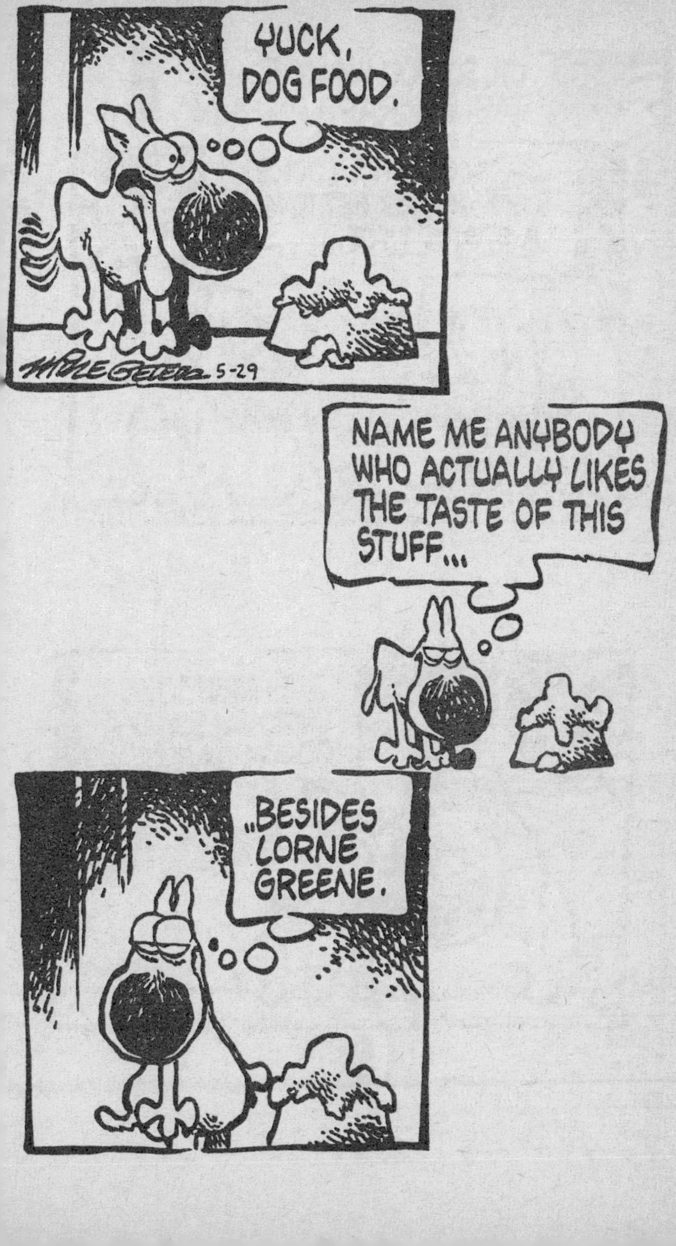
YUCK, DOG FOOD.
NAME ME ANYBODY WHO ACTUALLY LIKES THE TASTE OF THIS STUFF...
..BESIDES LORNE GREENE.

OH, OH, GRIMMY.. LOOKS LIKE YOU'RE GETTING A SPARE TIRE...
BUMP BUMP
SHE'S RIGHT.. TWO UNIROYALS AND A GOODYEAR, TO BE EXACT...BURP.
7/5

GRIMMY POSTER
ORDER FORM

NAME _____

ADDRESS _____

CITY _____ STATE _____ ZIP _____

DESIGN	QUANTITY	PRICE EA.	EXTENDED PRICE
NO TO STUDYING		4.95	
CRANK IT UP		4.95	
SURGEON GENERAL		4.95	
THINKING IMPAIRED		4.95	
SPECIAL OFFER ORDER ALL 4 FOR		15.95	

Postage & Handling $2 x _____ Items =

CT. Residents add 8% Sales Tax

TOTAL

☐ CHECK or MONEY ORDER ENCLOSED

☐ VISA   ☐ MASTERCARD

CARD NUMBER _____ EXP _____

SIGNATURE _____

SEND TO: **CLASS PUBLICATIONS**
            71 BARTHOLOMEW AVENUE
            HARTFORD, CT 06106

OR CALL 1-800-333-9999